PEABODY
MUSEUM
COLLECTIONS
SERIES

A Noble Pursuit

A NOBLE PURSUIT

The Duchess of Mecklenburg Collection from Iron Age Slovenia

Gloria Polizzotti Greis

Foreword by Peter S. Wells

Photographs by Hillel S. Burger

Rubie Watson, Series Editor

Peabody Museum Press, Harvard University

Editorial direction by Joan K. O'Donnell
Copy editing by Jane Kepp and Joan K. O'Donnell
Cover and text design by Kristina Kachele Design, llc
Composition by Kristina Kachele Design, llc
Color separations by iocolor, Seattle
Printed and bound in China by C&C Offset Printing Company, Ltd.

ISBN 0-87365-404-8

Library of Congress Cataloging-in-Publication Data:

Greis, Gloria Polizzotti.
A noble pursuit : the duchess of Mecklenburg collection from Iron Age Slovenia / Gloria Polizzotti Greis ; foreword by Peter S. Wells ; photographs by Hillel S. Burger.
p. cm.— (Peabody Museum collections series)
Includes bibliographical references.
ISBN 0-87365-404-8 (alk. paper)
1. Iron age—Slovenia. 2. Iron implements—Slovenia. 3. Antiquities, Prehistoric—Slovenia.
4. Slovenia—Antiquities—Collectors and collecting. 5. Marie, duchess of Mecklenburg-Schwerin, 1856–1929—Archaeological collections. I. Title. II. Series.
GN780.22.S57G74 2005
949.73'01—dc22

    2005029488

∞ The paper used in this publication meets the minimum requirements of the American National Standard for Information Sciences—Permanence of Paper for Printed Library Materials, ANSI Z39.48-1984.

FRONTISPIECE: The Vače Situla. This wine-mixing vessel, excavated at Vače, Slovenia, by the Duchess of Mecklenburg's uncle, Prince Ernst von Windischgrätz, is the cultural icon of the republic. Courtesy Narodni muzej Slovenije, Ljubljana, Slovenia. Photograph by Tomaž Lauko. See page 9 for a line drawing of the decoration on the situla.

Contents

Illustrations

PLATES

THE MECKLENBURG COLLECTION AND THE ARCHAEOLOGY OF IRON AGE EUROPE

Peter S. Wells

THE PEABODY MUSEUM'S Duchess of Mecklenburg Collection is a unique assemblage of European Iron Age material culture, excavated at the turn of the twentieth century by an unusual woman and finally brought to the attention of the wider world in the pages of this entertaining and informative account. The collection itself contains a representative body of objects from the southeast Alpine region of Slovenia, as well as items from twenty-six graves at Hallstatt in Upper Austria. These sites are places of vital importance to our understanding of Iron Age Europe as a whole.

The collection's many thousands of objects provide researchers not just with representative items of various types, but with multiple versions of bronze pins, bracelets, and belt plates; iron spearheads, swords, and axes; and glass and ceramic vessels. The materials come from sites that play major roles in scholarly debates about Europe in the Iron Age: primarily Magdalenska gora, Stična, and Vinica in Slovenia, and Hallstatt in Austria. Magdalenska gora, Stična, and Hallstatt are familiar to specialists in the European Iron Age; Vinica remains relatively unknown, a situation that will be redressed when the author of the present volume publishes the Mecklenburg materials from the site. Stična and Hallstatt have been subjects of significant recent investigations, and the materials excavated by the Duchess of Mecklenburg from these sites will continue to play a critical role in their interpretation. Hallstatt, in fact, is the "type site" of the Early Iron Age for the whole of Europe. This period, dating roughly 800 to 400 B.C., is frequently referred to as the "Hallstatt Period."

The Mecklenburg Collection is exceptionally well documented for graves excavated at the start of the twentieth century. During most of her excavations, the duchess had notes taken about the character of each grave and about the positions of the objects recovered. The Peabody's collection includes photographs of many of the mounds during excavation and of the contents of some graves. The duchess and her assistants kept the contents of each grave together, a practice not always followed by archaeologists of the time but one essential for retaining the integrity of each burial assemblage. The team of experts assembled in Zurich in the early 1930s to organize the objects, notes, and photographs also played an important role in preserving the high quality of the information. This exceptionally good documentation makes the Mecklenburg Collection of enduring scholarly value.

The Mecklenburg objects and their associations allow researchers to address a wide range of issues important to our understanding of the European Iron Age. This period is significant in relation to larger questions about human social and cultural development because these were the final centuries of "prehistory"—the time before Roman conquerors introduced the practice of writing to the lands north of the Mediterranean. The objects themselves permit analysis of technological processes applied to the production of iron, bronze, tin, gold, and glass. Specific types of objects, and associations between objects, allow study of differences in wealth and social status between members of the communities represented. Differences in the ways that women and men were buried make possible studies of gender distinctions in funerary ritual. Many objects have the character of amulets, allowing investigation of magic and superstition. Representations of animals and humans offer information about how people of the period viewed one another and the creatures that lived around them.

Trade is an important subject for understanding the changes that took place during the Iron Age, and interactions with other communities are well represented here.

Copper, probably from mines in the central Alps, and tin, from as yet unidentified sources, had to be imported to make bronze, which is abundant among the personal ornaments in the collection. Amber was carried across the continent from the Baltic region. Glass and ceramic vessels show connections to Mediterranean societies. Weapons provide insight into military technology in late prehistoric Europe. These and other issues of enduring interest to archaeologists and historians can be addressed through analysis of materials in the Mecklenburg Collection.

The duchess's connections with pioneers in the field of archaeology lend a special significance to the collection. The letters from Oscar Montelius and Joseph Déchelette attesting to their admiration of her working techniques are unique documents of this piece of archaeological history. They are augmented by photographs showing Montelius, the most prominent European archaeologist of his day, posed next to the duchess at her excavations at Stična (see p. 41).

The duchess was never formally trained in archaeology, yet her strong interest in developing the best possible techniques of excavation and recording led to major improvements in her working methods, resulting in the unusually fine documentation of her collection. She actively sought out advice from Europe's leading archaeologists and integrated their suggestions into her work. As Gloria Greis's account makes clear, the duchess was both energetic and determined, and she accomplished a great deal in the course of her decade of fieldwork. Readers familiar with European archaeology of the late nineteenth and early twentieth centuries will find particularly striking the many photographs of the duchess actually *excavating*—not just directing workers, as was the common practice of most archaeologists of her time. We see the duchess, often wearing an apron, sometimes posing next to exposed graves, sometimes hacking at the soil with a pick, sometimes on her knees scraping soil from around objects.

In *A Noble Pursuit*, Gloria Greis provides us with a tantalizing glimpse into the world of this fascinating woman and with a splendid—and beautifully illustrated—overview of the valuable and well-documented collection that she assembled. These objects from the European Iron Age will serve scholars of the future in their investigations into questions that have, as yet, not even been posed.

ACKNOWLEDGMENTS

NO SUBSTANTIAL BOOK PROJECT can be accomplished without the participation and cooperation of many people, even though the author gets to take the credit. I have always been fortunate in my colleagues, and I wish to express my gratitude for their invaluable assistance.

I am grateful to my former colleagues at the Peabody Museum at Harvard University who assisted in making available the Peabody's resources and collections: Rubie S. Watson, former director of the museum; Susan Haskell, curatorial associate for special projects; Hillel Burger, photographer; India Spartz, senior archivist; Patricia Kervick, associate archivist; Irene Good, Hrdy Research Curator; and Julie Brown, imaging services coordinator. Special thanks to Joan K. O'Donnell and Donna Dickerson of the Peabody Museum Press, who kept my nose to the grindstone, tied up all the loose ends, and generally kept everything moving forward.

Mildred Rendl Marcus generously provided funds to support the conservation of the objects illustrated in this volume through the Rendl Fund for the Conservation of Slavic Artifacts at the Peabody Museum.

I wish to thank Peter Wells, my graduate advisor in the Harvard University Department of Anthropology, now at the University of Minnesota, and the fellow students with whom I studied the Mecklenburg Collection for many years: Michael Geselowitz (Institute of Electrical and Electronics Engineers History Center, Rutgers University), Bettina Arnold (University of Wisconsin, Milwaukee), and Matthew L. Murray (University of Mississippi).

I thank Peter Wells, Rubie Watson, and Joan O'Donnell for their many helpful and valuable suggestions on the manuscript, Jane Kepp for her graceful editing, and Kristina Kachele for her lovely design.

Rainer-Maria Weiss, former curator at the Museum für Vor- und Frühgeschichte in Berlin (now director of the Helms Museums, Hamburg), first brought to my attention the wonderful rediscovery of the Stična Cuirass and has since provided me with information about his research on Kaiser Wilhelm II's Mecklenburg artifacts.

Ann Hörsell, of the Archives of the Swedish National Heritage Board, provided me with copies of the duchess's correspondence with Oscar Montelius and with permission to cite these letters in my work.

Several institutions and individuals provided me with photographs from their collections. I thank the Narodni muzej Slovenije, Ljubljana; the Museum für Völkerkunde, Berlin; and Matthew L. Murray, University of Mississippi, for their kind permission to reproduce these photos.

As always, love to my family—my husband, Michael Greis, and my children, Madeleine and Adam. Michael gets as excited about my projects as I do, but I still try in vain to impress the kids.

Finally, I was fortunate to work for many years at the Peabody with photographer Hillel (Steve) Burger. Steve's photos are masterpieces of light and clarity. He has been heard to claim (on more than one occasion) that his photos are often better than the real thing, and as much as I love the artifacts, I have to confess that he is sometimes right. Steve has now retired after thirty years at the museum, and I take it as a great honor that he came in after retirement to complete this project with me. I am pleased and proud that his photographs grace my book.

This book is dedicated to my good friend Steve Burger, with gratitude and love.

In the study of Antiquity (which is always accompanied with dignity and hath a certain resemblance to Eternity) there is a sweet food of the mind well befitting such as are of honest and noble disposition.
—*William Camden, English antiquarian and historian (1551–1623)*

A Noble Pursuit

Marie

Herzogin zu Mecklenburg Schwerin

Erinnerung an Dresden März. A.

1901

A New Science, a New Career

ARCHAEOLOGY AT THE START of the twentieth century was a new science. Indeed, the very idea of *pre*history was still relatively new. Since the seventeenth century, scholarly opinion about the age of mankind had been formed by the writings of James Ussher, archbishop of Armagh and vice-chancellor of Trinity College in Dublin. In 1654 Ussher had published *The Annals of the World,* a chronological treatment of world history in which he calculated the date of the Creation on the basis of the generations—the "begats"—in the Old Testament. By Ussher's reckoning, Creation began on Sunday, October 23, in the year 4004 B.C. Sir John Lightfoot, chancellor of Cambridge University, further refined the time to 9:00 A.M. Ussher was a respected and prominent churchman, and the unassailable authority of his scriptural sources, as well as the incorporation of his date into the Authorized Version of the Bible in 1701, guaranteed its widespread acceptance. The notion of "antiquity" was thus defined by two biblical events, the Creation and the Flood.

Marie von Windischgrätz, Duchess of Mecklenburg, circa 1900. This photograph was taken in Dresden and sent as a memento to her brother. Courtesy Matthew L. Murray, University of Mississippi.

The intellectual upheavals of the nineteenth century brought scholars to a new understanding of the history of the earth and mankind. Rationalist scientific inquiry began increasingly to reveal discrepancies between the biblical chronology and processes of change in the observed world. By the mid-nineteenth century, treatises such as Charles Lyell's *Principles of Geology* (1830–1833) and Charles Darwin's *The Origin of Species* (1859) had effectively demonstrated that the familiar geological and physical processes—erosion, accretion, the continuity of family traits—were uniform; that is, their mechanisms were unchanging. Thus, the earth and its creatures had not been fully formed in a single act of Creation but altered and transformed by innumerable incremental variations. By such a reckoning, the years of the earth had to number in the millions and not only a few thousand.

For archaeologists, the paradigm of geological succession became the principle of cultural succession. The new buried the old and was buried in its turn. The familiar mounds and relics in the landscape were understood to be the remains of predecessors rather than of lost antediluvian races. *Typologies* codified the formal characteristics of artifact types, and *chronologies* traced the changes in these typological traits over time. By the late nineteenth century, many of these regional chronologies and typologies could be linked to those of adjacent regions as archaeologists struggled to define broader patterns of cultural relationships.

The Mecklenburg Collection forms one component in this effort. The collection is named for its excavator, the Duchess Paul Friedrich of Mecklenburg (1856–1929), an Austro-Hungarian noblewoman and self-taught archaeologist. Between 1905 and 1914 she excavated at twenty-one sites, nearly all within her home region of Carniola. At the southwestern edge of the Austro-Hungarian Empire, Carniola (now the Kraijna) was roughly equivalent to the modern Republic of Slovenia.

The bulk of the duchess's collection now resides in the Peabody Museum of Archaeology and Ethnology at Harvard University. It comprises more than twenty thousand individual objects and forms the largest systematic collection of European antiquities outside of Europe.[1] Moreover, the collection retains much of its original documentation in the form of field notes written by the duchess and her secretary, numerous photographs of the excavations in progress, and letters to the duchess from

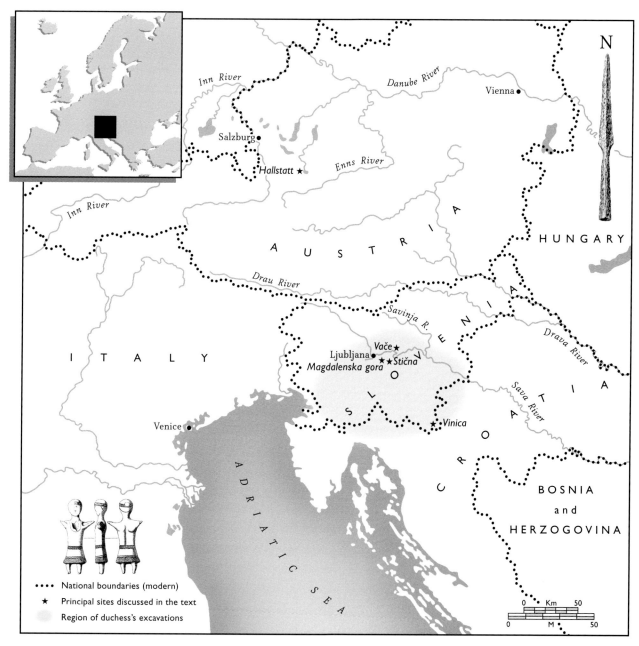

The region of the Duchess of Mecklenburg's excavations in Austria and Slovenia. The duchess excavated at twenty sites in the Austro-Hungarian province of Carniola (roughly, modern Slovenia) and at one site in Austria. Map by Deborah Reade.

her patrons and colleagues. The good documentation, along with the fact that the artifacts from each grave were kept together, enables modern researchers to derive from the collection valuable information about political and social change, gender and status differences, and trade and technology. The collection also contains many pieces that are unique in the central European art of this period.

How the duchess came to excavate this collection, and how it found its home in the Peabody Museum, is the subject of this story.

THE DUCHESS OF MECKLENBURG

Princess Marie Gabriele Ernestine Alexandra von Windischgrätz was born in Carniola in 1856, the youngest of the four children of Prince Hugo of Windischgrätz and Luise of Mecklenburg-Schwerin. At the age of twenty-five, Princess Marie married the Duke Paul Friedrich, her first cousin and the younger brother of the Grand Duke Friedrich Franz III of the German Duchy of Mecklenburg-Schwerin. The wedding was accomplished with some difficulty: although Princess Marie was a Roman Catholic, the wedding was performed at the Lutheran church in Schwerin without a Vatican dispensation. The Vatican challenged the legality of the marriage, providing the dispensation only after considerable delay and requiring the couple to marry again in a Catholic ceremony. In time, the duke and duchess had four children, two boys and two girls.

Their marriage, however, was not a happy one. The primary reason for the couple's estrangement seems to have been the duchess's incredible extravagance with money, which eventually caused even her very well-heeled family to object to her behavior. Such extravagance, when viewed in the context of the glittering imperial court, must have been truly breathtaking. According to the records of the Municipal Archives in Schwerin, the duchess was placed—at the insistence of her brother-in-law the grand duke and by a "mutual agreement" with her husband—under the guardianship of the civil authorities.[2] This was, in fact, a legal and financial separation from her husband; it took place sometime around 1900. A more colorful account of this incident is found in the memoir *The Berlin Court under William II* (1915), ostensibly the diaries of a court gentleman identified by the pseudonym Count Axel von Schwering:

... for it is said that, instead of making him a devoted wife, the princess indulged in such reckless extravagances that the grand duke had to interfere. Her father, however, succeeded in appeasing the irate grand duke, and since that time Duchess Marie has lived in a castle in Carniola, which she is not allowed to leave, with only a lady-in-waiting to keep her company. From time to time, Duke Paul pays her a visit, but otherwise she is forgotten by a world of which she is most fond.[3]

Count Axel was overstating his case. Although in disgrace, the duchess was not in fact a prisoner. She did attend court in Berlin on occasion, and did so in the company of her husband. Nevertheless, it is clear that by 1900 she was at a bit of a loose end. She was spending most of her time at her estate in Wagensberg,[4] the Windischgrätz home in Carniola; money was tight (at least by her standards); and she was lonely.

AN ARCHAEOLOGICAL CAREER

The Duchess of Mecklenburg first exhibited her interest in archaeology in 1905, when she was forty-eight. In April of that year she began conducting her own field excavations in the area around her Wagensberg home. Between April and November, more or less continuously, she excavated at nine different sites. No clear explanation can be found for this change in her life course. Archaeology, in the form of sponsoring someone else's excavations, was a frequent enough pastime for the European nobility. To be carrying out the fieldwork oneself, however, was hardly a common occupation for a middle-aged Austro-Hungarian princess. The duchess did not leave personal journals that might give researchers some insight into her thoughts, so her true motives cannot be known. Nevertheless, she suffered two painful losses in 1904—the death of her father, who had afforded her some legal and financial protection against her in-laws, and the death of her eldest son, Paul Friedrich, at the age of twenty-two. It was said that archaeology became her distraction from these sorrows.

But the question remains—why archaeology? The usual explanation is that archaeology was the family business, so to speak. The duchess's uncle, Prince Ernst von Windischgrätz, was a numismatist and archaeologist of considerable reputation in the

The duchess excavating. The Duchess of Mecklenburg took up archaeology in 1905, when she was forty-eight. Both her own family and that of her husband were interested in antiquities. Unlike most antiquarians among the nobility, the duchess conducted her excavations in person. Peabody Museum, Harvard University, photo T3709.1.

late nineteenth century. He was famous as the excavator of Vače, the geographic and sentimental center of Carniola. It was there that he discovered the famous Vače Situla, an exquisitely decorated bronze wine-mixing vessel now in the Narodni muzej (National Museum) in Ljubljana, Slovenia (see frontispiece).

Prince Ernst also maintained a private museum of his archaeological finds in his palace in Vienna. On her husband's side, the Mecklenburg–Schwerins were the founders of the Grand Ducal Museum in Schwerin, the first museum of antiquities in Germany to be organized systematically and chronologically. Thus, as a recent catalogue from Berlin's Museum für Vor- und Frühgeschichte observed, "the archaeological enthusiasm of both families apparently joined in the person of the Duchess Paul Friedrich. With such a familial tendency, it is hardly surprising that she developed right away a passion for archaeology. It is astonishing only that she was able to follow up her fervor for excavation and collection with such ambition, and with such personal and financial commitment."[5]

Prince Ernst may indeed have been the duchess's role model. Her first venture into fieldwork was at his Iron Age site of Vače.

The three tiers of decoration on the Vače Situla, a vessel of a type used in mixing wine (see frontispiece). The top register shows a parade of horsemen and charioteers. The second shows, on one side, a row of cloaked men being served drink by women with long, loose hair and by a hatless man holding a situla. On the other side, two men are boxing; between them stands their prize, a helmet with a long plume of horsehair, of the type illustrated in plate 20. The third register shows a line of deer, sheep, and rams followed by a hungry lioness. Throughout the registers appear sharp-beaked birds and a strange plant with a bifurcated leaf. Illustration from *Mittheilungen der Anthropologischen Gesellschaft in Wien* 1882, vol. 13, pl. xx.

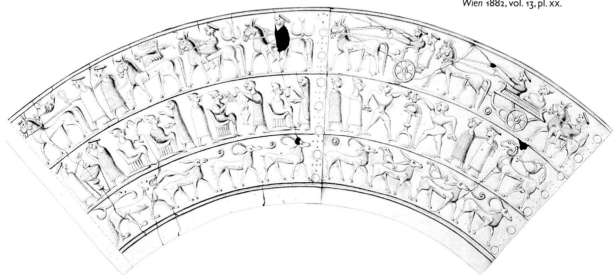

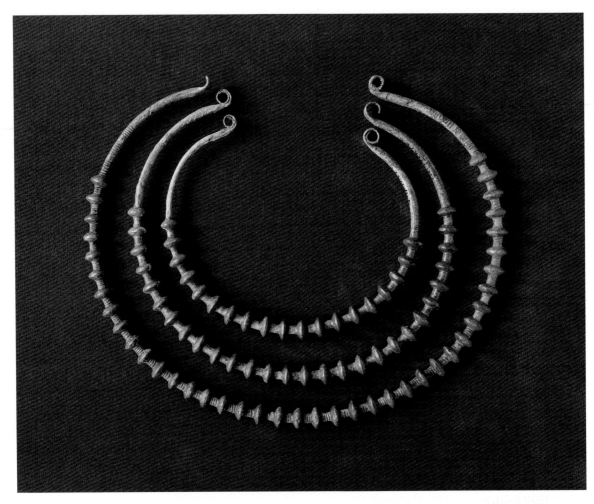

Three of the six bronze neck rings recovered from Magdalenska gora, Tumulus VII, Grave 40 (PM 34-25-40/14385.1–14385.3). T5141.2. Photo by Hillel S. Burger.

THE THREE AGES OF PREHISTORIC EUROPE

TO UNDERSTAND the importance of the duchess's archaeological work, one must understand something of the prehistory of central Europe. The broad chronological structures of European prehistory are the so-called Three Ages: the Stone Age, the Bronze Age, and the Iron Age. The Stone Age encompasses the millennia from the initial colonization of Europe by hominids nearly one million years ago through the development of settled village agriculture. Subdivisions within the Stone Age chronology mark the achievement of landmarks such as the appearance of modern *Homo sapiens sapiens* and the ability of humans to fashion stone tools of increasingly sophisticated form. The final phase, called the New Stone Age, or Neolithic (ca. 7500–1500 B.C.), was the time when agriculture replaced hunting as the main form of subsistence, and permanent village residence replaced seasonal transhumance.

The transition to the next period, the Bronze Age (ca. 1700–800 B.C.), was characterized by the widespread adoption of bronze, an alloy of copper and tin. Although native (naturally occurring) copper was known and used in the Neolithic, it was scarce. The technological breakthrough of the Bronze Age was the discovery of smelt-ing, a means of extracting copper and tin from their ores by melting the metal compo-nents out of their rock matrix. Although there were many sources of copper in Europe, the sources of tin were few, and tin ingots were traded over long distances. This technological advancement, therefore, first required changes in the social rela-tionships between territories that made long-distance trading partnerships possible. Bronze was valuable because it was costly to obtain and produce. Consequently, it was used more often for social, decorative, and ritual purposes, such as the making of ceremonial vessels and jewelry, than for utilitarian items such as tools and weapons.

IRON AGE HILL FORTS AND HAMLETS

The beginning of the Iron Age (ca. 800 B.C.–A.D. 1) saw the widespread adoption of iron technology. Unlike copper and tin ores, iron ores are abundant throughout Europe, but extracting the metal was difficult. The temperatures needed to smelt copper and tin were well within the reach of ancient pyrotechnology; the much higher temperatures needed to fully smelt iron were not. The partially smelted iron had to be forged—heated and hammered until the impurities were forced out. Forging remained the means of producing iron in Europe until the Industrial Revolution.

The introduction of iron did not displace the importance of bronze. People used iron primarily for tools and weapons, but bronze remained the more common and more valuable metal. This period of mixed use lasted for some four hundred years; archaeologists call it the Early Iron Age (ca. 800–400 B.C.). It is also known as the Hallstatt period, after the site of Hallstatt in Austria, where its characteristics were first defined.

The increasingly complex networks of social relations that began in the Bronze Age intensified in the Early Iron Age. Although long-distance trade was unnecessary for obtaining iron, the existing trade networks became the mechanisms for obtaining other goods and luxuries such as salt, amber, glass, horses, and raw materials.

The characteristic settlement type of the Iron Age was the hill fort, or fortified town. Within its ramparts lay the townspeople's residences, their household and communal storage structures, and their craft and manufacturing facilities. The slopes

Tumuli in the landscape around Stična, October 1913. The placement of the burial mounds in the twentieth-century landscape of farmhouses and grain fields was similar to their placement in ancient times, as can be seen in the map on page 39. Peabody Museum, Harvard University, photo S14363.

of the hill and the valley below provided pasture for grazing livestock and fields for growing crops. Surrounding the hill fort lay a hinterland of small towns and smaller agricultural hamlets that formed its productive support base.

Each hamlet or village probably contained no more than fifteen or twenty people—probably an extended family. Governance within the village was an extension of familial authority. The hill forts housed much larger groups. Hill forts were, by definition, the centers of political and economic control. In general, they were located at the edges of plateaus, overlooking the river valleys, which allowed them not only to control the agricultural land along their flanks but also to command the rivers as routes of commerce and communication. Stična, the largest hill fort known in this region, may have housed as many as 500 or 600 people, though the norm for hill forts in Carniola was probably 200 to 300.

These estimates of population are rough. Nevertheless, control over the hill fort population, and over the agricultural hinterland, rivers, and trade routes, must have exceeded the threshold of control possible in a kinship-based society. Social organization had shifted from its basis in the structure of the family to become the form known as a *chiefdom,* based on political, economic, and ritual control. A chiefdom can be broadly defined as a form of social organization in which centralized control is maintained over a territory. This power of control is invested in an individual, the chief, and is usually exercised from a central place, in this case a hill fort. The chief is responsible for regulating agricultural production and storage, for trade and commerce, and for defense. For the most part, chiefdoms were sustained by perceived reciprocal advantages: farmers and craftsmen provided their goods to support the chief, and chiefs provided commodities, famine relief in times of need, and defense.[6]

Scattered among the fields and villages were large *tumuli* (singular, *tumulus*), or burial mounds, that held and commemorated the dead. The placement of these mounds within the productive landscape attests to the ongoing role the dead played in the lives of the living. Burials proved the continuity of a family's residence in that place. Family burial monuments delineated family territory, and the mounds formed the tangible link between a lineage and its land. On a broader scale, these tumulus cemeteries marked and legitimated the boundaries of the territory controlled by the hill fort. Thus, the frontiers of the living were guarded by the armies of the dead.

The variety of imported materials at the hill fort sites is testimony to their control over the important trade routes. Some of the imports, such as fine pottery and ornaments, arrived as finished products. Others, such as amber and tin, were raw materials needed for goods produced at the site. The goods made from these materials would themselves be traded to other sites. In this way the hill fort elites ensured themselves and their people access to luxuries and augmented the productive resources of their territory by obtaining a broader range of raw materials than occurred naturally.

The character and importance of imported goods in central Europe changed significantly after about 600 B.C., with the settlement of the Athenian colony at Massalia (Marseilles). By establishing a trading entrepôt at the base of the Rhone, the Greeks gained access for the first time to territories beyond their traditional Mediterranean sphere of influence. In this new area the Greeks encountered the emerging chiefly class of the hill forts, a class eager to acquire the new luxuries the

Greeks had to offer. Olives, fine pottery, and wine from Greece became the new fashions in central Europe for those who could afford them (pls. 3, 4, 15); in return the Greeks gained the raw materials and livestock so scarce on their peninsula.

The addition of Greek imports to the trading system accelerated the social and political differentiation that had begun at the end of the Bronze Age. The growing desire to obtain Greek luxuries caused the hill fort elites to demand greater production of resources in their own territories, solidifying their social and political control. Greek imports, and the manners and customs that accompanied them, became the hallmarks of central European elite power in the Early Iron Age. This demand bolstered Greek power and extended Greece's influence throughout the Mediterranean world.

The Peloponnesian War (431–404 B.C.) put an end to Athens' colonial hegemony. After Athens fell in 404 B.C., Greek power in the Mediterranean quickly waned, leaving a political vacuum and a period of cultural upheaval that allowed several groups to expand territorially—notably the Celtic tribes out of central Europe and the Etruscans (and later the Romans) out of Italy. This upheaval also disrupted the old trade routes upon which the Early Iron Age towns depended. Consequently, many of the hill forts were abandoned or greatly reduced in size and power.

This period of unrest, which lasted until the Roman incursions of the first century B.C., is known as the Late Iron Age, also called the La Tène Period, after the site of La Tène in Switzerland. The Late Iron Age was the true Iron Age, in which the use of iron finally surpassed that of bronze.

GONE BUT NOT FORGOTTEN

In order to understand the European Iron Age (or the cultural history of any other part of the world), archaeologists seek data from many classes of remains—burials, domestic settlements, religious sites, manufacturing sites, and so forth. Each type of site contains its own characteristic classes of information. Domestic settlements, for example, provide data on the approximate size of the resident population and the organization of household and community units. Manufacturing sites tell of the group's level of technological attainment and of relationships with outside communities in the form of trade in finished goods and raw materials.

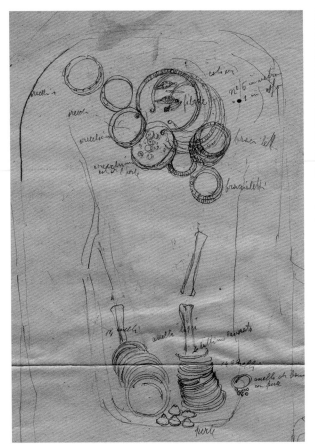 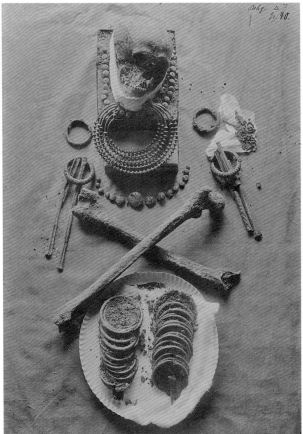

This field sketch of Grave 40 at Magdalenska gora, Tumulus VII, was made on August 28, 1913, by a Professor Torres, a visitor to the site. Because the grave was discovered and excavated at dusk, there was no time to photograph it or even to complete the hastily made sketch before darkness fell, so it shows only the main outlines of the burial. When the objects were transferred to Zurich in 1932, Adolf Mahr and his team photographed and inventoried them before they were put up for auction. The photograph at right shows the layout of objects on the museum shelf in Zurich: Mahr's attempt to reproduce the position of the body and the artifacts as they were originally found. Peabody Museum, Harvard University, 34-25-40/14627.1.1 (left) and photo S14380 (right).

Burials are a distinct class of archaeological data, traditionally one of the best studied and most abundant. The main characteristic of burials as data is that they are static. Settlements and manufacturing sites were dynamic; over the time of their use, new technologies replaced old, structures were pulled down and rebuilt, and fashions changed. Preservation of artifacts is typically poor on dynamic sites, because broken or lost objects were trampled underfoot and scattered, and refuse was swept away. In contrast, burials are time capsules. In Europe, they are what archaeologists refer to as "closed contexts"—that is, goods no longer move in or out, and the contents of the grave when excavated are the same (except for decay and incidents of plunder) as its contents when buried.

Burials are also usually the only context in which archaeologists meet an individual person and see the deceased as distinct from the aggregate of the community. The grave goods that attended a burial were usually objects associated with the deceased, and so they reflect that person's time and cultural identity. Within a cemetery, therefore, the abundance, value, quality, and character of the grave goods, when compared from one grave to another, delineate in tangible terms the hierarchy of social relationships. Broadly speaking, a wealthier person had more and better grave goods (pl. 22). Burial was thus the ultimate (in both senses) form of public representation. Through the quantity and quality of grave offerings, the identity of the dead person was carefully and meaningfully constructed to maximize the position he or she held both among those left behind in this life and among those who would be met in the next— a good last impression and a good first impression at the same time. The social position of the deceased (and, by extension, that of the survivors) was affirmed in terms of ritual conformity and adherence to group standards of social and material value.

Because of the relatively intact condition of burials, they were typically the favored sites for excavation in the early decades of archaeological science. Moreover, museums highly prized these cherished valuables as they shifted their focus from Classical to more local antiquarian treasures. The Duchess of Mecklenburg, as we will see, was no exception in seeking out burial sites as places to excavate.

Stična, Tumulus VII, under excavation in December 1913. The view shows the general method of excavation: slicing the tumulus vertically, trench by trench, from one edge to the other. Peabody Museum, Harvard University, 40-77-40/4626.1.

The Secret Stična Project

THE DUCHESS conducted her first excavation in 1905 at Vače, made famous a generation earlier by her uncle, Ernst von Windischgrätz. In the same year she excavated eight other Iron Age sites in the vicinity of her Wagensberg estates. (She excavated Iron Age sites almost exclusively.) These excavations were, for the most part, quite modest ventures, usually a single small tumulus or even just a single grave.

But despite the small scale of her excavations and her novice status, the duchess's early work attracted attention—and criticism—among archaeologists. Prince Ernst was a famous and respected antiquarian, so her family name was well known among prehistorians. Also, the eastern Hallstatt zone in which she excavated was emerging as an area of interest in European archaeology, and most antiquarian institutions were eager to acquire collections from the region. This zone, however, lay politically and culturally under Austrian control, limiting the access of museums outside of Austria. The duchess, with her high social standing and imperial relations, was in the right place at the right time. She had every intention of using this advantage to get what she wanted—and what she wanted was professional training and professional recognition.

In 1906 the duchess formed a plan to obtain both the training she wanted and the recognition she craved. During a stay with her husband in Berlin, she began arranging visits to the Prehistoric Department of the Königliche Museum für Völkerkunde (Royal Ethnographic Museum) in Berlin to indulge in a little shop-talk and to hint at the possibility of professional collaboration. She especially wanted the assistance of Alfred Götze, the keeper of antiquities for the Prehistoric Department, and of Friedrich Rathgen, their leading conservator. The director-general of the museum, Wilhelm von Bode, was in favor of this collaboration, making no secret of the fact that he saw in it the eventual likelihood of acquiring the duchess's collections for the Berlin Museum. Von Bode ordered Rathgen to Wagensberg with the admonition, "This collection would be an important enhancement to the Prehistoric Department, which from the East-Alpine region, and specifically the Hallstatt culture zone, holds nothing at all worth mentioning."[7]

Rathgen, for his part, did not want to go, and he acceded with little grace: "The duchess is starved for company in this isolated Wagensberg," he wrote back in complaint, "and holds onto everyone who is here for as long as possible."[8] His stated intention was to stay as briefly as he could; indeed, after only a few days he told the duchess that he was going back to Berlin. Annoyed by von Bode's mercenary support and Rathgen's obvious reluctance, the duchess declined to make over a single object to the museum, nor would she even reimburse Rathgen for his considerable travel expenses. Instead, she made a counteroffer: she would give the museum a tumulus of its own in the nearby Hallstatt-period cemetery of Stična, and Götze should come out to excavate it. Rathgen eagerly accepted this offer, which saved him from going back to Berlin empty-handed. An agreement was reached, and by the following week Götze had come out to dig. The so-called Secret Stična Project was under way.

The Stična Project was kept secret because Austrian law did not permit the export of antiquities without permission, and the Cultural Ministry was unlikely to grant such permission to its Berlin rival. Nor was the duchess eager to cause herself trouble in that quarter. As Rathgen wrote to von Bode: "The duchess wishes and believes without question that the excavation should be conducted under her name, so that she herself might maintain its secrecy from the gentlemen of the Vienna, Ljubljana, and other museums."[9] To prevent any unpleasantness with the Austrian museums, the story was given out that Götze was acting as an appraiser for the duchess and that the artifacts were being sent to Berlin only temporarily for restoration. The Austrian museums were so sensitive because they themselves had been attempting to get access to Stična for excavation but had met with little success. They were unable to gain the agreement of the local landowners and farmers, who objected to the destruction of their crops. The duchess succeeded because she was on her home ground and was willing to pay the farmer on whose land this tumulus lay nearly half his annual income for the use of his land.

The need for secrecy appealed to Götze's sense of cloak-and-dagger: "In order to avoid any scandal," he wrote to the duchess, "do not mention the excavations or the museum, and sign yourself only with your first name."[10] Thus, when Götze sent the duchess a telegram to expect his arrival, he carefully altered his signature from "Götze" to "Alfred," just in case it fell into the wrong hands. They were ultimately so successful at maintaining the secrecy of the Stična Project that the truth of the affair did not come to light for more than seventy years.

Götze did not wish to live at Wagensberg during the excavations—he was eager to avoid both the duchess and the long, bumpy drive between her palace and the site— so he moved into a guesthouse in the village of Stična for the duration of the project. His excavation method, common at the time, was to dig a trench along one edge of the mound and then cut back trench by trench, like slicing a loaf of bread. This yielded good information on the vertical relationships of the finds but was problematical for illustrating the plan of the finds, because the horizontal dimension was never exposed. Nevertheless, Götze made a good collection for the museum and was able to use this material to define the local chronology.

By staying in Stična, Götze expected not to see the duchess often. He was therefore more than a little disconcerted when she began showing up to work every day. She set up her own excavation at a mound beside Götze's, one that she had begun the previous year, and by watching and imitating his technique, she taught herself to excavate properly. Thus her plan was successful—she knew that the gentlemen of the Museum für Völkerkunde would not willingly tutor her, but she also knew that they would be

Magdalenska gora, Tumulus VIII, under excavation, August 20–28, 1913. The "steps" within the trenches allowed the excavators to expose the graves in plan view and record both their horizontal and vertical dimensions. The man in the soft hat (top, left) may be Gustav Goldberg. Peabody Museum, Harvard University, photo S14372.

unable to turn down the gift of a tumulus, so she set up a situation in which she could learn despite them. Finally, even Götze was impressed by her persistence:

> At any rate, the duchess has the most eager desire to use the scientific method, and the main idea is that she should be guided through her excavations, and allowed to go forward with the greatest thoroughness and accuracy. . . . If her excavations for lack of systematic technical training do not rise to the same level as those of trained archaeologists [meaning himself], still the reproach of grave-robbing is not justified.[11]

After 1906, the duchess's field technique improved dramatically. She acquired and trained an assistant of meticulous habits named Gustav Goldberg, whose job was to supervise the digs when she was away and to record the finds of the other fieldworkers while she was busy excavating her own features. She and Goldberg kept day-books of the excavations and recorded topography, grave associations, and the like. They made sketches and occasionally photographs of the features. Eventually the duchess solved the horizontal-plan problem by stepping back the trenches little by little, so grave assemblages could be exposed and recorded in their entirety before they were removed.[12]

Having thus acquired her "training," the duchess was eager to try her hand at more important projects. From July through December 1906 she undertook the first large-scale project of her career—the excavation of a La Tène–period (Late Iron Age) cemetery at Vinica.

The duchess excavating at Hallstatt, September–October 1907. She is assisted here by salt miners as well as by a few well-dressed visitors eager to try their hands at excavation. Peabody Museum, Harvard University, 40-77-40/4626.3.

Vinica and Hallstatt

VINICA LIES on the north bank of the Kupa River, which forms the border between Slovenia and Croatia. In the Late Iron Age, it was a settlement of a tribe known from Roman sources as the Iapodes, or Japodians. The Japodian territories were traditionally located to the south, on the border of Bosnia and Croatia, in the region of the Una Valley around Bihać. Vinica was the Japodians' northernmost settlement, an outpost probably achieved during the period of cultural upheaval that followed the Greek decline in the fourth century B.C.

AN ISOLATED OUTPOST

The rugged, mountainous territory of the Japodians was more difficult to reach than the regions surrounding it. The Dalmatian coast had seen extensive Greek settlement in the seventh and sixth centuries B.C. and, more recently, the establishment of Italian colonies. Northward, the region around Stična was already engaged in extensive trade with Rome, and the main trade route from Aquileia on the Italian Adriatic coast to

Emona (modern Ljubljana) and up into Austria was already in use. The Japodian area was cut off from these important trade routes by the Julian Alps to the north and from the coast by the formidable ridge of the Dinaric Alps; there was no easy access to the Adriatic in either direction.

Because of its rugged topography, the Japodian region was not generally suited to crop agriculture. The terrain was of heavy limestone karst, much of it intractable to the plow. The Japodians apparently maintained a pastoral economy based on the seasonal pasturage of sheep, supplemented by extensive hunting. They were known to produce good cheese and a hairy rather than woolly variety of textile too rough for anything but heavy outer garments.

The Japodians seem to have been noteworthy primarily for their isolationism. The borders between their territory and the land of the tribes to the north and east are fairly clear in both the archaeological and the historical records. In Classical sources the Japodians are generally distinguished from other tribes of the region, and they seem to have taken little part in the local political involvements that resulted from the rise of Roman power in the Adriatic and on the Greek peninsula. In archaeological sources they are invariably described as "conservative," assimilating some features of Late Iron Age La Tène style while retaining a significant proportion of earlier Hallstatt traits and local forms.

Of the Vinica settlement itself, little is known. The site is a hill fort enclosure, but no excavation has taken place within the hill fort itself. On the basis of comparison with similar hill forts known from the Japodian heartland farther south, some characteristics can be inferred. The site was not large, probably a couple of hundred meters in diameter. It was delineated by a single wall enclosing the hilltop. Unlike the settlements in the mountains to the south, Vinica (which means "vineyard") is located in a relatively open valley, more fertile and congenial than the main Japodian territory.

In the cemetery associated with the Vinica enclosure, the Duchess of Mecklenburg excavated a small number of Hallstatt-period tumuli, a flat cemetery of La Tène date that contained some 350 graves, and an early Roman cemetery nearby. No full plan of the Iron Age cemetery survives, but a partial plan made by Gustav Goldberg still exists. The graves were a mix of extended inhumations and cremations with and without urns. Judging from the burial population, the Early Iron Age occupation of Vinica was probably that of a small hamlet or extended family, and the Late Iron Age community consisted of probably no more than thirty people.

As a frontier outpost, Vinica seems to have been inward-looking even by Japodian standards. As at other Japodian sites, the artifact assemblage was a mixture of Hallstatt survivals coexisting with La Tène artifact types. In older chronologies this was sometimes referred to as the "Tardy Hallstatt" (pl. 21). It now seems clear, however, that unlike in the contiguous areas, where La Tène culture eventually replaced Hallstatt, aspects of La Tène style were selectively assimilated into Japodian culture and were used alongside the persistent earlier forms. For example, certain artifact types might occur together in a grave, although on the basis of their style they would be dated several centuries apart. Nevertheless, it is clear that the inhabitants of Vinica were familiar with the La Tène cultures of the northern Adriatic coast because of the large amount of glass and imported amber in the graves (pl. 6). The Vinica people also traded with the nomadic tribes to the east, and several classes of ornaments bear clear relationships to the art of the steppes (pls. 7, 8).

Vinica was also set apart from the other Japodian sites by several types of artifacts that are characteristic only of Vinica and occur nowhere else. Archaeologist Emil Vogt, keeper of antiquities for the Swiss National Museum, wrote a description of the Vinica artifacts in 1934 and offered the following opinion:

> Local Vinica taste is responsible for an evolution that led to grossly exaggerated baroque forms of somewhat rural exuberance. . . . A similar excessive growth for forms or details of forms is frequently met among cultures at the perimeter of (and sufficiently distant from) the big centers of civilization or which are otherwise sufficiently excluded to allow of such hypertrophia. A tendency of this kind characterizes practically the whole ornamental repertory of Vinica.[13]

The most striking examples are the so-called "anthropomorphic fibulae," or garment pins (singular *fibula*), in which the catch-plate forms the torso of a haloed figure (pl. 9). These are based on a regionally common type of three- or six-knobbed fibula, but they occur with this embellishment only at Vinica. The duchess found twenty-one such fibulae at Vinica, no two of which are alike. The idiosyncratic nature of the Vinica assemblage is most likely a symptom of the site's isolation. Culturally distinct from their neighbors to the north and geographically separated from their southern kin, the residents of Vinica seem to have taken cultural refuge in an exaggerated "Japodianness."

The Roman conquest of the Japodians by Octavian was accomplished in 35 B.C. with the defeat of the regional stronghold at Metullum (modern Melle, in Croatia). According to the Roman historian Appian, the Roman incursion inspired an ad hoc council to convene in response, but normally there was no centralized Japodian governing structure. Because of the lack of central leadership, the Japodians were unable to put up any concentrated opposition to the Romans, although regional fighting was fierce. The Romans found it difficult to reduce the hill forts because of problems in maintaining siege supplies over the inhospitable terrain, even though the actual distances to the Roman coastal bases were not great. After the conquest, the territory was divided between the new provinces of Dalmatia and Pannonia. The border was set along the Sava River for military considerations of strategy and pacification, rather than as any reflection of traditional or ethnic boundaries. Administratively, Vinica ended up in Pannonia, a province dominated by the peoples of the Hungarian Plain. Culturally, it was part of Dalmatia, like the rest of the Japodian lands. Among the older Iron Age graves at Vinica, the duchess excavated a number of Early Roman graves, which attest to this political and cultural transition (pls. 10, 13).

HALLSTATT

In the autumn of 1907 the duchess undertook a brief excavation at the site of Hallstatt in Austria. Hallstatt lies in the Salzkammergut, the mountainous region outside of Salzburg. It was the only site she excavated that was not within the boundaries of Carniola.

Hallstatt is one of the most famous sites in European archaeology and is the defining site for the Early Iron Age (ca. 800–400 B.C.). It sits atop a massive salt dome; this was a major salt-producing region in both prehistoric and historic times, a rich prize fought over repeatedly by invaders and princes.

An extensive cemetery for the Iron Age mining community was found and excavated between 1846 and 1863 by Johann Georg Ramsauer, then supervisor of the salt-mining operations. The burials were on the top of the mountain, surrounding the entrances to the shafts. The village associated with the cemetery has never been located.

Ramsauer excavated a total of 980 graves in what was the first extensive, systematic cemetery excavation in Europe. His careful and detailed work, preserved in a series of manuscripts and watercolors, set a new standard for archaeological recording.[14] Because of the large size of the database and the high quality of the documentation, the Hallstatt assemblage became the basis for the chronological definition of central Europe.

Yet Hallstatt was not a typical Iron Age settlement. During the Iron Age, as throughout most of European prehistory, local economies were based on farming. The economy of Hallstatt, by contrast, was industrial; it was one of the earliest sites of industry in Europe. Mineral salt from the mines was carried out of the difficult Hallstatt terrain along the rivers and traded perhaps as far away as Italy. Salt was a commodity of high value, both as a dietary necessity and because it was the only reliable means of preserving and storing food throughout the year. Coastal dwellers had easy access to sea salt, but inland people were forced to rely on the salt trade. The Hallstatt miners used their salt to trade not only for agricultural produce (there is little agricultural land in the Salzkammergut) but also for tools, raw materials, and luxury goods. Because of the great value of their salt, the miners were able to acquire an extraordinary range of imported goods. Artifacts found in the graves at Hallstatt display the greatest variety—in terms of material, type, and place of origin—of any Iron Age cemetery in Europe.

The Hallstatt cemetery is also unusual because its grave goods show that the standard of living was not only relatively high but also relatively uniform. By the Early Iron Age, most parts of Europe showed signs of political stratification, including the presence of a chiefly class with privileged access to luxuries and control over labor and production, distinct hierarchies in site layout and function, and inequalities in wealth. Such distinctions in rank are less strongly evident in the burials at Hallstatt and other salt-mining sites in the region. The burials contain valuable goods, but evidence for social distinctions between graves, in the form of differential distribution of those goods, is weak. Moreover, the skeletons found in these well-furnished graves show all the stress and damage attendant upon a hard life of labor in the mines. This suggests that the burials placed near the salt mines were those of the miners themselves and that mining was carried out as a system of freeholds for their own profit, rather than as labor for the benefit of an elite class.[15]

The duchess excavated at Hallstatt for about four weeks in September and October 1907. Her desire to dig there probably arose from its fame among archaeologists and its status as the "type site" of its period. Where better to announce herself as an archaeologist? She had some difficulty gaining permission at first; the Natur-historisches (Natural History) Museum in Vienna, which maintained the site, did not think highly of her archaeological activities and was reluctant to give her access. The duchess therefore sought and gained the support of her cousin, the Austro-Hungarian emperor Franz Josef, who later wrote in a letter to the duchess: "I learn with sincere satisfaction, through Your Highness's friendly letter, that the excavations in Hallstatt were indeed successful, and it makes me glad that I was able to contribute in some way to make this pleasure possible for you."[16] The emperor's backing gave the museum no choice but to accede to the duchess's request, but it did so with little grace. The first two locations in which it allowed her to excavate were barren; the third yielded graves, but on a much smaller scale than in areas excavated previously.

The duchess carried out her excavations at Hallstatt beset by the hostile attentions of her colleagues and local officials. Chief among these were Graf Salburg, the regional governor, whom the emperor had made responsible for arranging the necessary financing and permits, and Josef Szombathy, director of the Prehistory Department at the Naturhistorisches Museum. Although the duchess herself made notes about the excavations, a more interesting record of her work—and especially of the difficulties she faced—was made by Szombathy, who kept a diary during his visit to the site. From his diary, it is clear that these gentlemen had little regard for the duchess's skills as an archaeologist and that she had no high regard for them, either. He wrote: "The duchess has gone up to the mountain before 9 am, and will labor there well into evening. The son of [Vienna] museum curator Roth is her foreman, but she regards him with great mistrust and never lets his hands out of her sight for a moment. So far she has found only odds and ends."[17]

The duchess initially employed twenty-two laborers from the saltworks to assist with the excavation. The workers were pleased because she paid a higher wage than the mines, but their absence began to hurt the production of salt, and many were ordered back to their usual toil. By the third week, she was able to employ only eleven miners, but she supplemented her workforce by hiring the younger members of the local councilor's staff.

Despite his disdain for her skills, Szombathy—like Götze before him—was impressed by the duchess's dedication. She spent long days on the mountain and excavated with her own hands. He was also forced to admit that her graves, though less rich and spectacular than Ramsauer's, yielded some very fine artifacts (pls. 11, 12). In all, she excavated some forty-five graves at Hallstatt.

Through a combination of persistence and imperial kinship, the duchess succeeded in achieving the first of her goals, professional training. The Berlin and Vienna museums, central Europe's premiere archaeological institutions, had been made to accommodate her archaeological ambitions. Although they did not like her, they could no longer ignore her.

Stična, Tumulus V, in the course of excavation, October 1913. The generous allowance provided by Kaiser Wilhelm II allowed the duchess to hire whole villages as her fieldworkers. Peabody Museum, Harvard University, photo N33275.

A New Patron

WITH THE EXCAVATIONS at Stična, Vinica, and Hallstatt, the duchess was dedicating most of her time to her archaeological fieldwork. Her excavations were extensive, and she employed an army of fieldworkers. In 1906 she was in the field for seven months, and in 1907, for more than six months. In 1908, however, she excavated for only two and a half months, and in 1909, not at all. She spent only two weeks in the field in 1910, and only four days in 1911. The duchess had run out of money. Her excavations were expensive. Money for the 1906 and 1907 seasons had probably come from her own resources, with some help from the emperor; when Franz Josef helped her to gain access to Hallstatt, his assistance included a disbursement from the treasury. But as 1912 arrived, the duchess was broke and in need of a patron. She turned in this extremity to another imperial cousin, Kaiser Wilhelm II of Germany.

This was a calculated move. The kaiser took a keen interest in antiquities and fancied himself an accomplished archaeologist, sponsoring the German excavations on Corfu. He maintained a museum of antiquities, especially of arms and armor, in his

Kaiser Wilhelm II of Germany visiting his excavations at Corfu. The kaiser (in cloak and boots, center) was an enthusiastic amateur archaeologist and sponsored excavations at Corfu for many years. He also maintained a museum of ancient arms and armor at his palace in Berlin. From Griesa and Weiss 1999, *Hallstattzeit*, p. 61. Courtesy Bildarchiv Preussischer Kulturbesitz/Art Resource, NY.

Berlin palace. The duchess believed she could exploit their mutual interest in archaeology to persuade the kaiser to provide her with financial support for her excavations.
Although she had no publications of her own excavations, she sent him an article by
Ferdinand von Hochstetter entitled "Recent Excavations from Vače and St. Margaret
in Carniola in the Hallstatt Period," by which she intended to introduce him to the
work she was doing and spark his interest.[18] The kaiser was indeed interested, but
knowing her spendthrift tendencies he was also reluctant to send the duchess money.
So she made a more tempting offer—she began to send him some of her best finds for
his collection. The strategy worked: by June 1912 she was in the field again at Stična.

The following spring, the duchess found the most spectacular object of any that she
would excavate, the so-called Stična Cuirass, a gilded bronze breastplate made in the
Greek style.[19] She excavated the cuirass in mid-April 1913, and by late June she had

The Stična Cuirass. This cuirass is, without question, the finest artifact the duchess excavated. Made of sheet bronze in the Greek style, it is modeled in the characteristic form to represent a bare torso. The cuirass was once gilded over its outer surface, and patches of gilding still survive in places. When worn, the front and back plates would have been connected by straps at the shoulders and by lacing along the sides. As Rainer-Maria Weiss, former curator at Berlin's Museum für Vor- und Frühgeschichte, has pointed out, this armor was functional as well as beautiful. A flange at the collar protected the neck. The large armholes allowed for freedom of movement, and the outflaring skirt permitted the wearer to ride a horse. This photograph shows the cuirass as it appears today, fully restored and on display at the Museum für Vor- und Frühgeschichte in Berlin. From Griesa and Weiss 1999, *Hallstattzeit*, p. 68. Courtesy Bildarchiv Preussischer Kulturbesitz/Art Resource, NY.

sent Gustav Goldberg to the kaiser in Hamburg with the gift. The timing of Goldberg's journey was carefully chosen. Each year in July the kaiser left on his yacht from the port of Hamburg for a month-long North Sea cruise; this *Nordlandreise* was the highlight of his year. By sending the crates to the kaiser in Hamburg on the eve of his departure, the duchess counted on finding him in a good mood.[20]

Her hunch paid off. A week after Goldberg's arrival in Hamburg with the crates, the kaiser sent the duchess a letter:

> Please accept my sincerest thanks for your splendid gift! Goldberg arrived safely here with the treasure. Treasure it is and quite unique. Professor Schuchardt was present and was perfectly amazed at the phenomenal splendor of the cuirass. He declared it to be an "unicum," the finest of its sort that was ever found. . . . I make you my compliments at this absolutely unique find which you may be proud of, and at the same time I am deeply touched that you, Dearest Cousin, have so graciously thought of me and sent me this splendid gift. . . . I have ordered my [private secretary] Grimm to place himself in communication with you through the bank—which you kindly name—and to pay out to you through the bank 100,000 marks for *your excavations.*

Carl Schuchardt was the director of the Berlin Museum für Völkerkunde, succeeding Wilhelm von Bode in 1908. He often advised both the kaiser and the duchess on archaeological matters, and he acted as curator for the kaiser's own collections, where the cuirass became one of the highlights. One hundred thousand marks was worth approximately $1.2 million in current value.

But the kaiser still had reservations about giving the duchess money. His letter went on:

> This sum is to be used *solely* for *your work,* and to enable you to do it fully, without the necessity to live about in Hotels and Towns, thereby losing money and time; the money is solely for this Research and the advancement of Science, and the acquisition on behalf of the Giver of the most beautiful and most outstanding

The duchess's winter camp at Stična, December 22, 1913. The duchess stayed in the field as long as possible and returned home just in time for Christmas. She is just visible in her broad-brimmed hat at the entrance to the large tent on the right. Peabody Museum, Harvard University, photo T3713.

objects that might be found; but it is not to be used for any other purpose! . . . once more my very best and warmest thanks and every wish for renewed and successful work, of which I consider myself the *Geistliche Inspirator und Leiter* [spiritual inspiration and leader] and in which I take the keenest interest! [21]

The kaiser need not have worried. Finally solvent, the duchess spent over nine months in the field in 1913, by far her most productive year. In the course of it she excavated as many graves as she had excavated in all previous years combined, camping on site even as winter descended and not returning home until Christmas Eve. Her methods of excavation, developed over the years since the Secret Stična Project, were as systematic and scientific as any practiced in Europe at the time. Thanks to the kaiser's substantial financial support, she could be as extravagant in her archaeological pursuits as she had once been in her clothing and jewels. She hired whole villages as her fieldworkers. She hired an artist to draw and paint grave plans and sections as well as artifacts (pl. 19). She acquired a camera and used it to record the excavation of each tumulus and the major grave deposits. Although she had made some photographs in previous years, the photographic record starting in 1913 is remarkable, with images numbering in the hundreds.[22]

STIČNA

Upon returning to the field in 1912, the duchess concentrated her efforts on the Early Iron Age sites of Stična and Magdalenska gora. These two sites marked the high point of her archaeological career and represent the best of her scientific work. Better still, at these two sites she finally gained the long–sought recognition and respect of her archaeological colleagues.

Stična lies in the foothills some thirty kilometers southeast of the modern Slovene capital of Ljubljana. It was a hill fort, a large hilltop settlement surrounded by a rampart of stone and earth. Its enclosed area measured approximately eight hundred by four hundred meters, making it the largest hill fort known from this region. The hill fort was subdivided by a long interior wall running from east to west along the center of the enclosure; another wall formed a small "corral" on the western edge. The main rampart was pierced by several gates around the perimeter. Stična was occupied for about two hundred years, from roughly 625 to 425 B.C.

Filling the landscape to the south of Stična were large grave mounds, some 140 of which are still extant, though many more have eroded or been destroyed in the twenty–five hundred years since they were built. Tumulus construction was labor intensive, and so a mound was intended to hold the numerous burials of an extended family or kin group. A typical mound at Stična was about forty meters in diameter and rimmed by a low wall of stone. In the earlier part of the Early Iron Age, these mounds were organized around an important central burial, and additional burials were added around the perimeter over time. In the later part of the Early Iron Age, the central burial became less important and was often absent, and all graves were arranged around the perimeter. As new graves were added, new layers of earth were mounded onto the tumulus, so that it grew larger over time. The tumuli at Stična contained an average of seventeen graves each, incorporated over the span of a century or so.

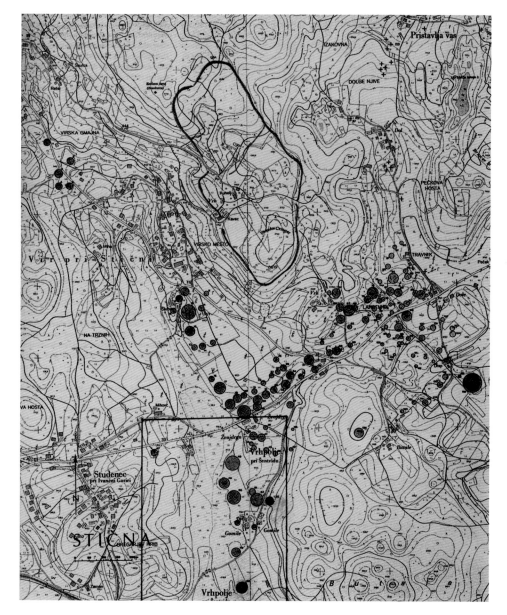

Modern topographic map of the hill fort at Stična and its environs. The hatched line indicates the ramparts, with three "gates" and two interior walls still visible. The shaded circles represent the roughly 140 tumuli that survive around the site. The duchess excavated eleven of these. From Griesa and Weiss 1999, *Hallstattzeit*, p. 53. Courtesy Bildarchiv Preussischer Kulturbesitz/ Art Resource, NY.

The duchess conducted the first intensive fieldwork ever done at Stična, and little additional work took place there until after the Second World War. Beginning in the 1950s, the Narodni muzej in Ljubljana carried out an extensive campaign of excavation at Stična and throughout Slovenia, compiling a rich database of Early Iron Age sites in the region.

The duchess began her work at Stična on a small scale in 1905 and then resumed with Götze in 1906. Her most extensive work at the site, however, took place between 1912 and 1914, after she received funding from the kaiser. At Stična she excavated eleven tumuli containing a total of 186 graves. It was her good fortune to find the site relatively intact and well preserved: in 1845 the Commission for the Historical Association of Carniola had declared the mounds to be of natural rather than man-made origin, and so the site had escaped the notice of treasure hunters long after neighboring sites had been plundered.

The duchess employed a large crew to excavate at Stična. Goldberg's detailed notes contain lists of the workers' names and the rate they were paid; in the second week of March 1913, for example, the duchess employed sixteen men at 2.2 marks per day, about $24 in current value, and sixteen women at 1.7 marks, or about $20. Despite the large crew, the work was carried out with care and precision. The duchess and Goldberg kept day-books recording the contents, layout, and description of each grave. The services of both an artist and a photographer were retained to make visual records. The objects were labeled and packed together to maintain the integrity of each grave group.

The highlight of the duchess's career came in the second week of October 1913 with the visit of Joseph Déchelette and Oscar Montelius to her excavations at Stična. Montelius, the Swedish minister of antiquities, was unquestionably the preeminent European archaeologist of his day, and Déchelette was one of the leading archaeologists in France. Shortly after a visit to the duchess, Déchelette wrote to his colleague Saloman Reinach, curator of the Musée des Antiquités Nationales in St. Germain-en-Laye:

Oscar Montelius visiting the excavations at Stična, October 1913. Montelius (with suit and hat, center) was the Swedish minister of antiquities and the preeminent European archaeologist of his day. Joseph Déchelette, the leading archaeologist in France, was also visiting but is not shown in the photograph. Much impressed by what they saw at Stična, Montelius and Déchelette carried favorable reports back to their colleagues and to the kaiser, who was financing the duchess's excavations. Peabody Museum, Harvard University, photo T3710.

I have returned from Wagensberg, that picturesque summer residence of the Duchess of Mecklenburg in Carniola. Her archaeological work is truly admirable. One hears everywhere in Germany and Austria that the tumuli are being destroyed, in that they are excavated without method. This is absolutely false. In truth, hardly anyone else spends so much care in the conduct of the work that neither artifacts nor important observations are allowed to be lost. Montelius, who has seen the excavations, shares my opinion entirely.[23]

Both men delivered academic papers about the duchess's excavations shortly thereafter.[24] Their visit, and especially the endorsement they provided to their colleagues after seeing her excavations, finally established the duchess's credibility as an archaeologist. Upon his return to Roanne, Déchelette wrote to her:

I see in my mind's eye this admirable collection where all of the objects have their ordered place, which gives them a very particular value. I cannot understand how in the presence of such magnificent results your detractors, motivated by a low jealousy, can have tried to cast discredit on this admirable scientific work that Your Highness has pursued with such perseverance and disinterest, in spite of all the material and other difficulties. But the results are there to quiet their lies.[25]

The duchess continued to send the kaiser objects for his museum, and he in turn continued to send money. In October 1913 she sent him another large crate, this time using Montelius as courier. Sending Montelius rather than Goldberg was a deliberate bid to maintain Wilhelm's interest in her work. The kaiser had great admiration for Montelius, and the duchess knew that the authority of his testimony would negate any of the criticism by her professional rivals in Berlin that might have reached the kaiser's ears. Montelius, who genuinely admired the duchess's archaeological work, was willing to perform this service. In the few days preceding his visit to Wilhelm, the duchess sent Montelius a flurry of telegrams in which she laid out her strategy in her somewhat idiosyncratic English:

Ask you most ardently to follow this desire. Is of greatest importance that you see him and tell the so very important things, the more so as he is going to Schoenbrunn [Franz Josef's palace in Vienna] on the 22nd filled with the impression of what he has heard from you. Future works depend entirely upon your conversation with him. [October 13]

All my thoughts tomorrow and on 17th with you in Bonn. Put my whole confidence in the ardour and *chevalresque enthusiasme* of your words if you speak of enormous quantity of workmen that such gigantic work requires. Would dispense of entering into numbers but I am happy to say that with most energetic address and raising pay have happily obtained about the huge numbers wanted. Do everything to avoid that somebody is sent to help and assist me for doubtless it would absolutely compromise my future works. [October 15]

Wrote him [the kaiser] how you look forward with greatest interest to hear his *auffassung* [opinion] about the girdle–belt [decorated belt plate] as you yourself are not quite fixed of real signification and that you consider object of highest importance the more so being quite unique. Envy you of intense joy discussing interesting subject with him. Please write detailed description of all. [October 16] [26]

Montelius did send the duchess back a long letter on the evening after the visit, describing his meeting with the kaiser ("He was quite a charming fellow") and recounting the rigors of his journey with the large crate in rather comic terms. As she had hoped, he was an enthusiastic advocate for her work to the kaiser:

He looked over the things you sent with the greatest interest. . . . The belt plate he found especially valuable. I said that I was very curious to learn what he thought about it, and he seemed to be of the opinion that the animal [depicted on it] should be seen as representing a god rather than a votive offering.

The photographs he regarded as something remarkable. I said that I had not expected to find so many photographs of the graves . . . and that I—like Déchelette—have come to regard the excavations and their results with admiration. Your excavations are not only *much* better made than most in those regions, but they are also conducted in a truly scientific and methodological manner. . . . I explained how you carry out the work with military order, as you remove only a small amount each time, so that nothing should get lost. I also explained many other things about your exemplary management of the work. I especially emphasized that you had arranged for an artist to come, to make plans of the mound and the various graves, and a profile to make clear the position of the graves to each other.

I also said that *this* method of investigating a tumulus costs a *great deal* of money, and that it is of the greatest importance not only for you, but also for [the advancement of] Science that you can continue to conduct your work without hindrance. A foreigner, I said, could not achieve as much as you had, because he does not know the people or have the same relationship with them that you do. I also said that you owe it to his powerful patronage that you have been able to continue your very valuable work.

Speaking of your great energy, I said something that he perhaps dismissed as flattery but was nevertheless meant truly. I said, "One can see that the Duchess is indeed a kinswoman of Your Majesty."[27]

Relieved that the visit went so well, the duchess poured out her thanks and frustrations in a telegram the following day:

Find no words to express deep thankfulness for your extreme amiability, to have gone to Bonn guided by noble feelings of *gerechtigkeit* [justice], having seen how unjustly my work has been discredited by calumnies of people inspired by base feelings of jealousy, *enttäuschte* [thwarted] ambition, and other unnoble motives. Emperor sent me quite charming telegram after having seen you. Am happy that His

Majesty invited you to lunch and was so charming and amiable. Hope soon to receive your letter and that all these voyages have not fatigued you too much.[28]

The kaiser sent the duchess an enthusiastic letter of thanks in February 1914. Her beautiful objects were becoming the highlights of his Berlin display cases:

> The descriptions you make of your work, the difficulties of the climate, the soil, the joys and disappointments varying at the different discoveries, read like a romance. It takes a great deal of genuine "archaeological" enthusiasm to brave such climatical difficulties, as you have done! Your life in the tent must have been most trying and reminds me of descriptions of voyagers to the Pole! I am looking forward with the *greatest interest* to the transmissal of the five helmets, etc. . . . I stand up for archaeology and sincere honest labor and will be proud to sing your praise before my filling "vitrines"! When can I expect the objects? As soon as you need a sum let me know how and where to send it.[29]

In March, Secretary Grimm sent the duchess another bank draft for 100,000 marks.

The care with which the duchess excavated and documented her finds makes the Stična collection useful for analysis even after nearly a century. For example, the variety of imports at Stična attests to the scope of its trading network. Baltic amber, which was abundant at the site, was prized both for its beauty and its amuletic power. Iron and copper were locally available, but the tin needed to make copper into bronze was rare and might have reached Stična from Austria or Italy. The glass, though locally produced, incorporated valuable constituents such as cobalt blue that came from outside Stična, possibly from Asia Minor. Horses were obtained from the nomads of the Eurasian steppes.[30]

The elites of Stična also enjoyed the fashionable luxury of Greek wine and had adopted the elaborate social rituals that went with drinking and serving it. The equipment associated with wine included not only drinking vessels of specifically Greek types but also locally made and imported vessels for mixing wine with water before serving it, according to the Greek practice.[31]

The Stična grave goods point out certain demographic patterns that are borne out by the larger database from more recent excavations by the Narodni muzej. Iron, in the form of weapons, occurred only in the graves of adult males. The typical suite of weapons consisted of a pair of spears, an ax, a knife, and a heavy bronze belt plate to protect the midriff. During the later Bronze Age, the typical male weapon had been the sword, a weapon intended for open, hand-to-hand fighting. The Early Iron Age shift to spears and axes reflected a shift to the Greek style of fighting in close formation—a style that became both more fashionable and more pragmatic as Greek power reached across the Mediterranean. Men's graves contained little bronze other than defensive accouterments: the fittings and plates for the belt, bridle trappings for horses, and, in rare cases, helmets.

Iron was rare in the graves of women and children. Female graves were rich in personal adornments and domestic implements, such as glass and amber beads (pls. 18, 19), decorated bronze dress pins, bracelets, and other jewelry (pls. 24, 25), and spindle whorls (which might have functioned as amulets as well as tools). These characteristic "female" grave goods were placed not only in the graves of adult women but also in those of all preadolescent children, regardless of gender. This suggests that the society recognized a right of passage that conferred adult status on males.

On the basis of the relative quantities of grave goods, some distinctions can be made regarding the social status of individuals. It is generally assumed, for Stična as elsewhere, that the wealthier or more important people were buried with greater quantities of high-value grave goods. It is also generally assumed that burials with few grave goods belonged to people with less wealth or perhaps lower social standing. This assumption can be partly supported by the observation that the very wealthy graves at Stična occurred in tumuli that generally contained other well-furnished graves—that is, those of a wealthy family—just as the graves with the least goods tended to occur together. Nevertheless, such evaluations of wealth can really be made only at the extreme ends of the scale. For the broad middle of the range, such analyses are plagued by inadequate models for discerning comparative value, leaving many important questions unanswered—for example, how to compare the wealth of women and men or the protective power of amulets over that of weapons, as well as the vexed issue of quantity of goods versus quality of goods.

MAGDALENSKA GORA

The second great site the duchess excavated with the support of Kaiser Wilhelm was Magdalenska gora. She had worked there briefly in 1905 and again sporadically from 1906 to 1908, but the majority of her work took place in 1913. Overall, she excavated ten tumuli containing 355 graves.

Magdalenska gora lies some ten kilometers west of Stična. It is a much smaller site, an oval hilltop embankment measuring about 125 by 225 meters. No major internal partitions remain visible; there is a single opening in the rampart to the south. About forty tumuli survive around the site, spread out to the west and north along the rivers. Magdalenska gora was occupied slightly later than Stična, approximately 600–300 B.C., and was in use for a longer time. Nevertheless, the sites were contemporaneous for most of their history and fulfilled similar social, economic, and political functions. Much of the foregoing discussion of Stična applies to both sites.

Despite the sites' overall similarity, some significant differences exist between Stična and Magdalenska gora. The most apparent lies in the density of burials within the tumuli: at Stična, tumuli contained an average of seventeen graves, whereas at Magdalenska gora the average was thirty-six. Magdalenska gora yielded a greater number of weapon-bearing graves, and they included a greater number of personal items (pls. 14, 16, 23). The Magdalenska gora graves were generally more richly furnished than the Stična graves: there were more objects per grave (pl. 22) and a greater number of high-status objects such as helmets (pl. 20), horses (pl. 1), and bronze cauldrons and other drinking and wine vessels. The overall impression is of a community that was wealthier, more masculine, and more warlike than Stična. The "warrior" character of the Magdalenska gora assemblage might have reflected just a cultural preference in representation, or it might have reflected real-world political concerns in the fifth century, as Greek power in the Mediterranean declined and the Etruscan and Celtic tribes began to expand out of their Italian and German homelands.

The duchess excavating at Magdalenska gora, August 1913. Peabody Museum, Harvard University, photo T3711.1.

The Great War
and Its Aftermath

IN 1913, as her discoveries began to accumulate, the Duchess of Mecklenburg began for the first time to think about publishing her work. For this task, she turned (on Joseph Déchelette's advice) to David Viollier, director of the Musée National Suisse and an expert on the Hallstatt period. She first contacted Viollier in October 1913; he expressed his desire to carry out the project but noted that existing obligations would prevent his starting until the following year.

That time would never arrive. On June 28, 1914, Archduke Franz Ferdinand, heir to the Austrian throne, was assassinated by Serbian nationalists in Sarajevo. As July progressed, each major European power was drawn into the conflict, and by August 5 all of Europe was at war. Déchelette, although over fifty, volunteered for service and was killed in the opening months of the war. Astonishingly, despite the growing hostilities, the duchess went back to Stična on July 28. Her work there lasted just over a week before she abandoned the attempt; it was her last excavation. In her nine-year career she had excavated some twenty thousand objects from more than a thousand graves at twenty-one sites.

The duchess spent the war years in Berlin, taking care of the kaiser's collections and compiling an album of photographs and a catalogue. After the war she returned home to Wagensberg—no longer in Carniola, but now part of the new Kingdom of Serbia, Croatia, and Slovenia. Most of her family property had been confiscated; her archaeological collections, which had been kept at Wagensberg and which filled seventy-two crates, were taken to the Narodni muzej (National Museum) in Ljubljana.

The duchess spent her remaining years at Wagensberg, petitioning the new King Alexander for the return of her collections. She died impoverished on July 9, 1929, a few weeks before the confiscation order was finally rescinded.

THE AUCTION

The duchess's collection was restored to her daughter, Marie Antoinette, and the crates were returned to Wagensberg. Marie Antoinette immediately sought permission to sell the collection outside the country, arguing that it was the only asset left to her. The Narodni muzej opposed the sale, but the young duchess persuaded the king to allow it to proceed. The Narodni muzej was nevertheless allowed to keep a representative selection of the artifacts for its collections.[32] In 1932, Marie Antoinette handed the remainder over to Anderson Galleries, a prominent New York dealer in fine arts, to prepare the artifacts for auction.

Anderson's was eager to handle the sale but faced the problem of how to make the material attractive to its audience. The gallery usually dealt in expensive European paintings, Asian antiques, and the like, and an archaeological collection such as this one, which had not yet even been cleaned of dirt from the field, was unfamiliar to its clients. In order to enhance the value of the collection, Anderson's hired a team of experts—a *Who's Who* of central European Iron Age specialists—to prepare the artifacts for sale. Under the direction of Adolf Mahr of the National Museum of Ireland, the team members gathered in Zurich, where they unpacked the artifacts, laid them on shelves to make sure the field notes and object records agreed, organized the photographs and field documentation, and partitioned the material into auction lots (see figure on p. 16). Anderson's also commissioned Mahr's team to write the sale catalogue. The resulting volume, *Prehistoric Grave Material from Carniola,* remains a classic reference for the archaeology of the region.[33]

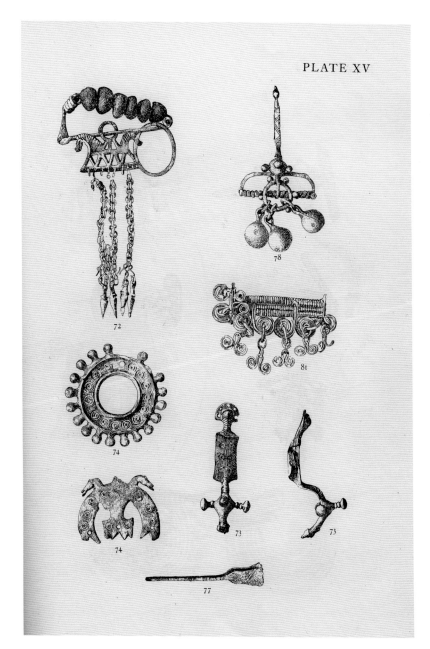

PLATE XV

72

78

74

81

74

73

73

77

Plate 15 from the *Prehistoric Grave Material from Carniola* catalogue. In an effort to promote interest in the sale of the Mecklenburg Collection, New York's Anderson Galleries commissioned some of the leading archaeologists in Europe to write the sale catalogue. Highlighting the text were numerous engraved and photographic illustrations of the artifacts. Several of the items illustrated here appear in plates 2 and 9 of the present volume. The bronze pendant designated no. 81 in this illustration (PM 40-77-40/11362 from Vinica, Grave 165) is made from numerous small wire spirals. Although its meaning is unknown to us, the spiral was a powerful image throughout Europe from earliest prehistory. Courtesy Tozzer Library, Harvard University.

In 1933, as the sale approached, Anderson's agents began contacting their clients. In this way the sale came to the attention of Hugh Hencken, curator of later European prehistory at Harvard's Peabody Museum of Archaeology and Ethnology. Hencken heard about the sale while in London. Usually a man of few words, he tore off a letter to the Peabody's director, Donald Scott, that covered thirty-one pages of Royal Hibernian Hotel stationery, making his case for pursuing the collection: "It is the type of material that if it were to be excavated today would never be allowed to come to America. . . . Nothing like it has ever come before to our country and never will again. . . . I know that you will agree that no stone should be left unturned to acquire at least a part of this great collection."[34]

Hencken knew that the purchase of the collection was beyond the means of the Peabody or any other single museum. Europe and the United States were in the depths of the Great Depression, and there was no realistic hope of raising the $250,000 that Marie Antoinette sought. Hencken feared that the collection would be sold off piecemeal into private hands and be lost to study. He tried instead to assemble a consortium of American and European museums to buy shares and to cooperate in the analysis and publication of the collection. His effort failed. The European museums were too short of funds to participate, and the American museums, with little experience of European archaeology, were uninterested.

Anderson's, for its part, touted the collection as the "Carniola Treasure" and took out full-page ads in glossy magazines such as *Art and Archaeology:* "No such important event has transpired before in this country in the sale of antiquities bearing on prehistory, and the thorough documentation of the objects in the sale assures not only their intrinsic scientific value, but the addition of letters and holograph documents from imperial personages and noted scholars adds a touch of romance often lacking in such instances."[35]

Despite its best efforts, Anderson Galleries was unable to interest its customers in the collection. The sale day, December 1, 1934, came and went. Hencken was then able to approach Marie Antoinette's own agent with the Peabody's offer. Although the funds were small, he succeeded in purchasing the material from Magdalenska gora, about one-quarter of the collection. The Ashmolean Museum at Oxford University purchased one lot containing a situla and other arti-facts from the duchess's excavations at Vače. The remainder went into the Anderson warehouses.

During the next few years, the financial condition of Anderson Galleries grew increasingly precarious. Finally, the owners, sensing irregularities, sought to replace their treasurer. He, as it turned out, had been falsifying the books, embezzling funds and art-works from the company and from clients. In order to avoid discovery, he took out an insurance policy on his erstwhile successor and then hired a thug to murder him. The attempt failed, the thug identified his employer, and the treasurer avoided prosecution by committing suicide. The scandal covered the front page of the *New York Times* for days, and what little was left of Anderson Galleries was placed in receiv-ership. As the remaining assets were liquidated, Hencken convinced the supervising judge to sell the remainder of the collection to the Peabody for the small sum the museum was able to amass on short notice, rather than simply to discard it.

THE MECKLENBURG COLLECTION TODAY

Older archaeological collections often languish in museums as newer, more "scientific" collections displace them. Happily, this fate has never overtaken the Mecklenburg Collection. It is well known among European archaeologists; that it is not known more widely is perhaps due to the troubled history of the twentieth century. If the duchess and Viollier had succeeded in publishing the collection while it was

Hugh Hencken. Hencken was curator of later European prehistory at the Peabody Museum, Harvard University, from 1930 until 1979. His primary area of research was the pre-Roman cultures of Adriatic Europe, though he also conducted research in North Africa and northern Europe. Hencken heard about the sale of the Mecklenburg Collection during a gallery trip to London in 1933. He immediately recognized the scientific importance of the collection and ultimately obtained it for the Peabody Museum. Photograph by Bachrach.

The Stična Cuirass on display in Berlin. This photograph was first published in 1935 in an article about princely graves in central Europe. The cuirass, from Stična, Tumulus IV, Grave 30, is displayed with a double-crested helmet from Magdalenska gora, Tumulus VII, Grave 39. The helmet was also excavated by the Duchess of Mecklenburg, who gave it to Kaiser Wilhelm for his museum. Both artifacts were looted after World War II but were recovered when Germany was reunified in 1993. Peabody Museum, Harvard University, photo T3705.

still intact, their book would likely have ranked among the classics of its time. As it stands, the upheavals of two world wars and the vagaries of the confiscation and sale have clearly caused both artifacts and documentation to be lost. The saddest loss, surely, is that of the renderings and sections made by the hired artist. There is a photograph of him at his easel, and a few artifact illustrations survive to attest to his skill. Had his grave illustrations survived, they would no doubt have been both informative and beautiful.

Yet despite its age and complex history, the collection remains valuable for research. Hencken, after many years of research on the collection and related materials, published *The Iron Age Cemetery of Magdalenska gora in Slovenia* (1978), laying out the definitive chronology of the region on the basis of the finds from Magdalenska gora. Hencken's successor at the Peabody, Peter Wells, published *The Emergence of an Iron Age Economy: The Mecklenburg Grave Groups from Hallstatt and Stična* in 1981. In it he used the artifacts as the basis for demonstrating the role played by trade and technology in the development of political hierarchies during the Hallstatt period. Subsequent researchers have used the collection to study the sociopolitical significance of changes in the techniques of iron production and to trace the networks of the amber and glass trade, among other things. Because of its great size and the high quality of its documentation, the collection remains a valued database even as scholars focus on new topics of inquiry.

The research potential of the Mecklenburg Collection is far from expended, and much work remains to be done. The large component from Vinica, for example, has not yet been published, leaving an unfilled gap in our understanding of the Late Iron Age in the Kraijna. Vinica is particularly important because, unlike the numerous Hallstatt-period sites from this region, La Tène–period sites are scarce, and excavated sites of the Japodian culture are few. The situation is especially dire in Croatia, where warfare throughout the twentieth century has caused widespread destruction of sites and cultural repositories.[36]

The most interesting development in the recent history of the Mecklenburg Collection has been the return of Kaiser Wilhelm's collection to Berlin. The kaiser's Berlin palace, where he maintained a museum of arms and armor, was stormed and looted during the brief socialist uprising that followed his abdication in 1918. Carl Schuchardt saved the kaiser's antiquities collections—including the Stična Cuirass—by removing them for safekeeping to the Museum für Völkerkunde, where they remained during the 1920s and 1930s. They were finally lost in the widespread looting that followed the fall of Berlin in 1945. The reunification of Germany in 1990 brought parts of the collection again to light. Although the complete facts are not known, it seems that the collection was taken into the eastern zone after the partitioning of Berlin, and from there eventually to Leningrad. After about thirty years the artifacts were sent to repositories in the East German city of Leipzig, where they remained until German reunification. Rainer-Maria Weiss, former curator at the Museum für Vor- und Frühgeschichte in Berlin, spent several years establishing the historical provenance of these finds, among them several fine helmets from Stična and Magdalenska gora and the wonderful Stična Cuirass.[37] Although many of the kaiser's archaeological treasures have yet to be found, many that had been given up for lost are again available for study and admiration.

The Duchess of Mecklenburg would have been pleased by the scholarly attention paid to her collection. Throughout her brief career she struggled for credibility as an archaeologist, and to this end she sacrificed her wealth, her time, and her comfort. But why? She was by no means an unconventional person in most other aspects of her life. She did not noticeably chafe against the restricted role of women in the early twentieth century. Nor was she rebelling against her class. Titled, wealthy, and pampered, she was happy to take full advantage of the perquisites of her rank. What, then, were her motives for taking up the practice of archaeology, her fierce determination not only to pursue but to succeed in a profession both so obscure and so masculine? However well studied, the Mecklenburg Collection will never resolve this one impenetrable mystery.

Color Plates

PLATE 1

Bridle ornament in the shape
of four horses' heads
34-25-40/8550
Magdalenska gora,
Tumulus V, Grave 31
Cast pewter (lead and tin)
Length 4.8 cm, width 4.7 cm

THIS ORNAMENT, a swastika formed of four horses' heads, probably dates to the fifth century B.C. It is made from an alloy of tin and lead. Three such ornaments were found at Magdalenska gora.

Most likely the ornament was not made at Magdalenska gora but was imported as part of the horse trade. Both its form and its material are characteristic of the Scythians, the famed equestrian nomads of the eastern steppes. The tribes of southeastern Europe traded with the nomads for their excellent horses, which were taller and stronger than the central European ponies. This ornament once decorated a harness and no doubt accompanied a horse that was exchanged for salt, glass, bronze, or iron. Many of the artifacts associated with horse bridles at Stična and Magdalenska gora were of Scythian rather than local origin.

The horse-head swastika is a symbol of great antiquity in western Asia. It saw widespread use throughout the nomad territories, and examples have been found in Romania, Bulgaria, and Russia as well as Slovenia. The swastika was a benevolent symbol; the term itself derives from the Sanskrit word for "well-being." It is thought to represent the sun and its quarterly manifestations—the cardinal directions and the migration of the seasons. (T5139.2. Hillel S. Burger, photographer.)

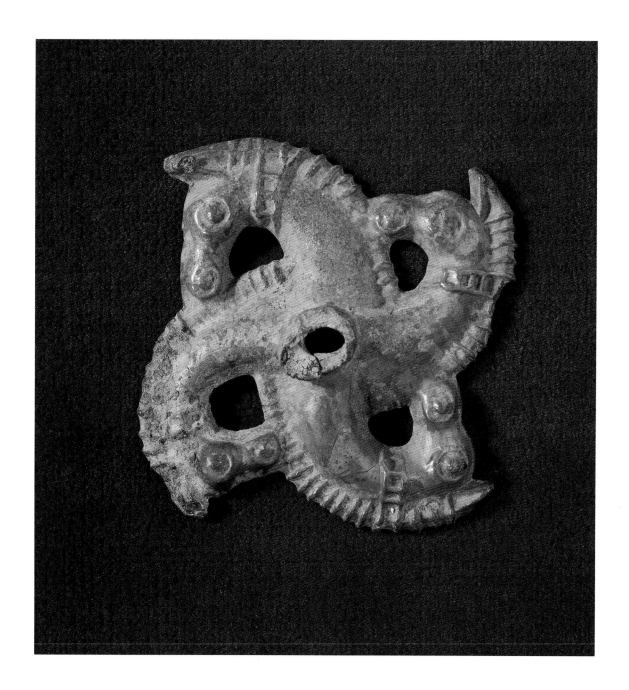

THE VINICA PORTION of the Mecklenburg Collection is notable for its abundance of jewelry and relative scarcity of weapons and tools. The jewelry is often of elaborate design, incorporating amulets and charms. Most of the amulets fall into one of three categories: anthropomorphic (human form), zoomorphic (animal form), or geometric. They usually take the form of pendants or beads and may appear as decoration on a functional item, such as a fibula (cloak pin) or belt plate. In a world full of threatening and mysterious forces, these charms were thought to have an independent spirit that could influence events in favor of the wearer. Such charms acted not against a specific evil but against a range of perceived dangers. We do not know if they were placed in graves because the deceased had worn them in life or for a particular purpose after death; certainly, some of them seem too heavy or unwieldy for everyday wear.

The two ornaments depicted here are typical of the jewelry found at Vinica (for other examples, see pls. 6–9). Both are elaborate fibulae from which hang decorative pendants that would have jingled and rung as the wearer moved. The sound itself might have afforded the wearer protection. (Opposite: T5119.2; left: T5072.1. Hillel S. Burger, photographer.)

PLATE 3
Bronze cauldron with
zoomorphic handles
40-77-40/13684
Stična, Tumulus VI, Grave 8
Sheet bronze body, cast bronze
handles and straps
Diameter 28 cm, height 12.5 cm

CAULDRONS MADE OF SHEET BRONZE were treasured possessions that betokened the owner's wealth and high status. Like situlae, cauldrons were made in imitation of Greek vessel forms and were used in the rituals associated with drinking wine. Their value derived in part, therefore, from their association with Greek luxury. They also had great intrinsic value because their manufacture required a large amount of costly bronze and great skill on the part of the artisans who shaped them.

Cauldrons were frequently decorated with incised designs around the rim. The cruciform straps that hold the handles are typical of those on bronze cauldrons from this area. The handles themselves have twisted shafts and turned-up ends that resemble the heads of ducks or geese. Below is an artist's rendering of a similar cauldron recovered from Tumulus II, Grave 3, at Stična (Wells 1981, *The Emergence of an Iron Age Economy*, fig. 37). (T4969.1. Hillel S. Burger, photographer.)

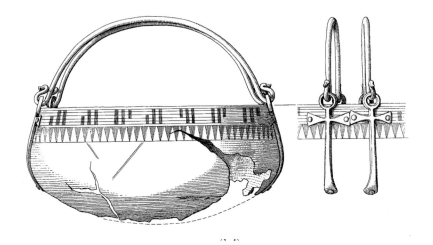

PLATE 4
Rhyton in the form of a ram's head
40-77-40/13526
Stična, Tumulus IV, Grave 47
Clay, oxide(?) pigment
Length 20 cm, height 16 cm

ALONG WITH VESSELS in which wine was mixed and served, there were vessels from which it was drunk. These two drinking cups from Stična, though of different origins, are both of characteristic Greek form.

The ram's-headed drinking horn, known as a *rhyton,* was filled from the open top, and liquid flowed out from a small hole in the ram's mouth. A rhyton has no base and no stopper; its contents flow as soon as it is filled and must be drunk all at once. This rhyton is made of buff-colored clay, with traces of black decoration. Analysis of the clay indicates that it was made in a Greek workshop in the eastern Adriatic, probably in the fourth or third century B.C. It is thus one of the few wine vessels in the collection that can be definitively identified as an import from the Greek world. The grave in which it was found also contained the bones of a sacrificed horse, another sign of the owner's wealth and high status.

The flat, shallow cup below is a *kylix.* Supported by a pedestal base, it allowed for more refined and contemplative appreciation of the wine. Its surface, now worn and eroded, was once decorated with a palmate design in thick black paint. Analysis of the buff-colored clay shows that it was probably made in a provincial Greek workshop and not on the Attic peninsula. (Opposite: T5062.1; below: T5061.1. Hillel S. Burger, photographer.)

Kylix, wheel thrown, decorated
with palmate motif in black slip
40-77-40/13189
Stična, Tumulus II, Grave 7
Clay, oxide(?) pigment
Diameter 13.5 cm, height 6.5 cm

PLATE 5
Scabbard plate with
geometric design
40-77-40/10088
Vinica, Grave 2
Cast bronze, iron rivet
Length 16 cm, maximum width 5 cm

THESE SCABBARD PLATES of cast bronze are both decorated with animal designs, though one is naturalistic and the other more abstract. The five-sided plate below bears a clear image of a running stag, with large antlers and the characteristic protruding tongue. The trapezoidal plate opposite has a geometric design down the center, but the linear designs at the edges terminate in animals' heads.

Knives were the most useful and versatile of implements. Unlike axes and spears, they served not only as weapons but also as general-purpose household tools. They were often encased in scabbards of leather or another soft material, which were reinforced and given structure by plates such as these. The elaborate decorations of these scabbard plates no doubt also had significance as charms or amulets. The plates therefore conferred both tangible and intangible benefits, protecting the knives and the men who wore them. (Opposite: T5150.1; below: T3719. Hillel S. Burger, photographer.)

Scabbard plate with
image of running stag
40-77-40/10366
Vinica, Grave 35
Cast bronze
Length 9.6 cm, width 4.3 cm

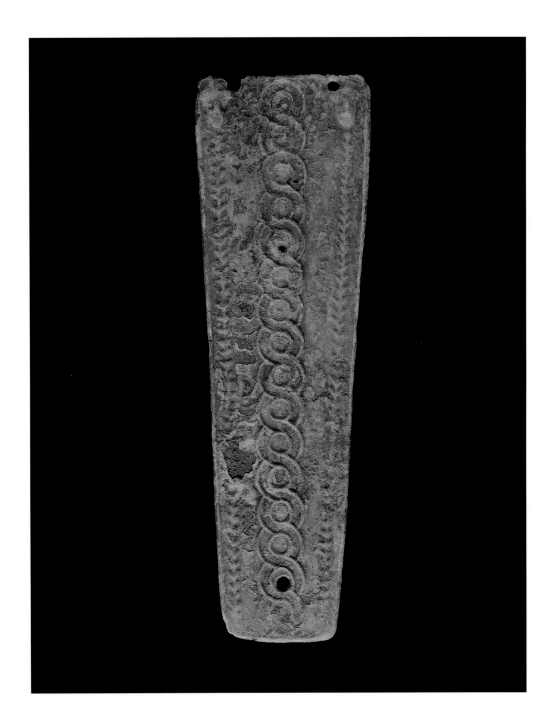

A FIBULA, OR COILED CLOAK PIN, is made by the same method as a modern safety pin. The pin's shaft leads to a coiled spring, which provides the tension. The part that extends from the spring and runs across the top—the part that is visible when the pin is in use—is called the bow. The bow terminates in a hook, or catch-plate, in which the point of the pin rests when the fibula is closed. Because the bow was visible against the cloth, it was usually the most highly decorated part of the fibula.

The beautiful fibula shown here was made in several pieces. The spring is very wide, to support the weight of the fibula. The true bow, which is not visible, is a narrow flat strap to which the visible (false) bow is attached. The false bow is inset with a piece of yellow glass, a fragment from a broken glass bracelet of a type made locally. At the front is a false spring that serves no function other than to offer visual balance to the true spring. Attached to the false spring is a pair of bulls' heads (see inset).

The elaborate decoration of this fibula did not enhance its function; indeed, it detracted from it. The weight of the additional decoration put strain on the spring, which had to be reinforced with a small iron rod (visible as rust at the end of the coil). Nevertheless, for the wearer and the observer, this piece was laden with social and symbolic meaning. Prehistoric Europeans had no written language, so information about an individual and the social and cultural groups to which he or she belonged had to be transmitted through a visual code, which archaeologists refer to as *style*. Style is the material manifestation of one's personal and social allegiances. Every visual detail of the fibula—the bulls, the yellow glass of the bow, the double spring, the massive size—would have had its significance in placing the wearer within his or her ritual, regional, and social context. (Opposite: T5135.2; inset: T5127.2. Hillel S. Burger, photographer.)

PLATE 7
**Bronze pendant depicting
two serpents**
40-77-40/12205
Vinica, Grave 268
Cast bronze
Length 11 cm, width 7 cm

THIS OPENWORK BRONZE PENDANT is a classic example of the double image. Seen from the edges looking toward the center, it appears to be two serpents or dragons, coiled back-to-back, with wide round eyes and open jaws. Seen from the center line, it is a single human figure whose hands grasp fighting serpents. It might even be a figure formed from (being transformed into?) serpents.

This dual image of the serpent-man probably originated in the art of the western Asian steppes and came to Europe through trade with nomads. It appears frequently in Iron Age art throughout Europe. Although the depictions vary from object to object, they all contain certain details in common—the central position of the human figure, the mirror-image symmetry of the serpents, and their circular eyes and open, birdlike beaks.

This double image was long-lived in European art. Some of the most interesting examples of the serpent-man figure date well after the Iron Age, into the Anglo-Saxon and early Christian periods of northwestern Europe, around A.D. 500 and later. The famous gold purse lid from Sutton Hoo (England) depicts a version of this figure. In early Christian contexts the X-shaped human in the center often becomes a cross, and the serpents are turned into open-mouthed fish, the Greek name for which is an anagram for *Christ*. (T5132.1. Hillel S. Burger, photographer.)

PLATE 8
Double fibula with double
horse-headed pendant,
decorated with incised triangles
40-77-40/10658
Vinica, Grave 74
Cast bronze
Length 11.5 cm, width 16 cm

PENDANTS IN THE FORM of double-headed horses were common zoomorphic amulets at Vinica. This motif, too, was derived from the animal-style art of the Asian steppes. These pendants usually consist of a pair of trapezoidal plates that terminate in their upper corners with the heads of horses facing in opposite directions. The plates themselves are decorated with incised triangles or circles. In some forms (see pl. 2), the body of the pendant is perforated with openwork triangles, suggesting the legs of the horses. In Asian forms, a central figure sits astride the horses. At Vinica, the central figure has been attenuated into the loop from which the pendant was suspended. The plates are finished with a row of bells or pendants that jingled when the wearer moved. The concentric "eye" design is common on such pendants and also had amuletic significance.

The pendant from Grave 212 (below left) is unusual for its degree of realistic detail. A small rider is mounted on each horse, and each rider wears a plumed helmet similar to those depicted on the Vače Situla (see frontispiece and the illustration on p. 9). The riders' legs are visible in relief on the plate. Replacing the usual triangular jinglers is a row of boots with turned-up toes. Because items of dress are so rarely depicted in Iron Age art, this charming little pendant is also a valuable source of information. (Opposite: T5145.2; below left: T3714; below right: T5134.1. Hillel S. Burger, photographer.)

Horse-headed pendant
with helmeted riders and
pendants in the shape of boots
40-77-40/11733
Vinica, Grave 212
Cast bronze
Width 6.5 cm, height 7 cm

Double horse-headed pendant,
decorated with incised eye motif
40-77-40/11542 (top), 11543 (bottom)
Vinica, Grave 196
Cast bronze
Width 11 cm, height approx. 11 cm

PLATE 9

Anthropomorphic fibula with
perforated halo and wire "earring"
40-77-40/10763
Vinica, Grave 90
Cast bronze, iron rivets
Length 15 cm, width 4.3 cm

SO-CALLED ANTHROPOMORPHIC FIBULAE are those on which the catch-plate forms the torso of what appears to be a "human" figure, often haloed. They are based on a regionally common type of knobbed fibula but occur with this figural embellishment only at Vinica. The Duchess of Mecklenburg collected twenty-one such fibulae at Vinica, no two of them exactly alike.

Although they are called anthropomorphic, it is doubtful whether the small figures on the catch-plates are in fact human. Their features are depicted with varying degrees of precision, but nearly all have wide, staring eyes and a halo around their heads. Even in the Iron Age, the halo signified a deity or at least a magical being. (Opposite: T5133.1; below left: T5079.1; below right: T5103.2. Hillel S. Burger, photographer.)

Anthropomorphic fibula with
figure of a snake crawling up
the torso
40-77-40/10573
Vinica, Grave 65A
Cast bronze
Length 11.5 cm, width 4 cm

Anthropomorphic fibula with
halo and wire earrings
40-77-40/11429
Vinica, Grave 180
Cast bronze, iron pin
Length 13.5 cm, width 4 cm

Roman-style bronze belt buckle
with repoussé ornament depicting
an equestrian figure
40-77-40/12583
Vinica-Podklanč, Grave 328
Sheet and cast bronze, iron rivets
Length 5 cm, width 4.3 cm

THE OCCUPATION AT VINICA spanned the period of the Roman conquest of the Adriatic and the establishment of the Roman provinces of Pannonia and Dalmatia. As part of the pacification of these provinces, the Romans, eager to minimize chances for a successful rebellion, relocated hill fort settlements such as Vinica to the river valleys. The valley settlements were harder for the native tribes to fortify and defend, and proximity to the rivers facilitated the Romans' access to their supply lines.

Reflecting this shift in settlement, the former residents of Vinica established a new cemetery at Podklanč, two kilometers from the original Vinica cemetery. The Podklanč burials, from which these objects came, contained not only the familiar Vinica forms but also increasing numbers of Roman-style artifacts, including glass vessels (see pl. 13), fibulae with hinges rather than springs (below), and belt buckles. (Opposite: T5073.1; below: T5138.2. Hillel S. Burger, photographer.)

Two Roman-style hinged fibulae
40-77-40/12577 (left) and
40-77-40/12578 (right)
Vinica-Podklanč, Grave 325
Cast bronze, bronze wire
Length 7.5 cm, width 2.7 cm;
length 5 cm, width 2.7 cm

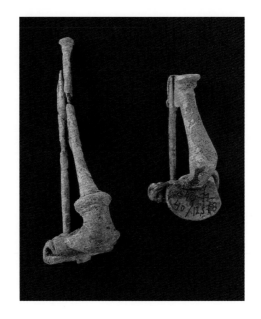

PLATE 11
Stepped bowl, interior decorated
with incised geometric design
and coating of graphite
40-77-40/9950
Hallstatt, Grave 21
Clay, graphite
Diameter 39.4 cm

ONE OF THE CHANGES that marked the advent of the Hallstatt culture was in the style of pottery. Before Hallstatt times, Bronze Age pottery in central Europe was usually thick walled, with incised or modeled decoration. The Hallstatt style was characterized by broad open forms, thinner walls, and decoration in geometric designs executed in red oxide paint or silver–gray graphite. (Opposite: T5124.1; below left: T5122.2; below right: T5121. Hillel S. Burger, photographer.)

Ceramic bowl, exterior
surface decorated with red
slip and graphite
40-77-40/9938
Hallstatt, Grave 23
Clay, iron oxide pigment, graphite
Maximum diameter 22 cm,
height 12.5 cm

Ceramic jar, exterior surface
decorated with red slip and
graphite
40-77-40/9949
Hallstatt, Grave 21
Clay, iron oxide pigment, graphite
Maximum diameter 18 cm,
height 14 cm

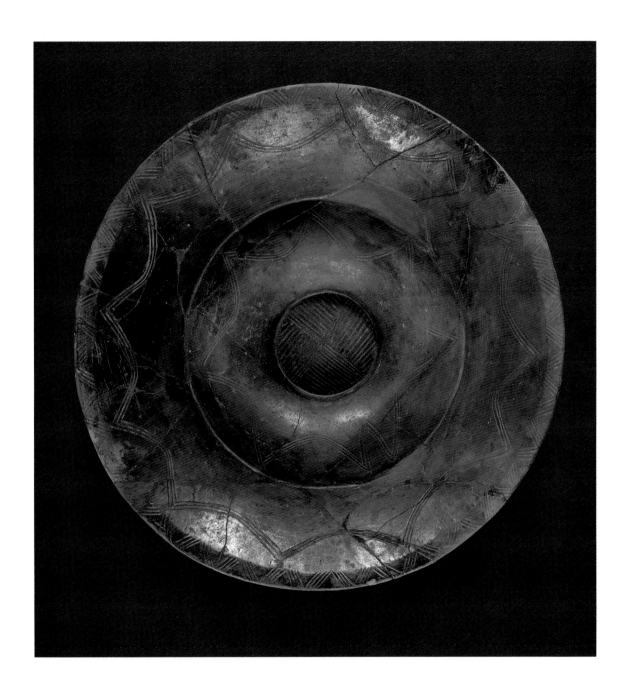

PLATE 12
Bronze figurine of a bull
40-77-40/9896
Hallstatt, Grave 12
Cast bronze
Length 14.5 cm, height 7 cm

AT HALLSTATT the duchess excavated this exquisite figure of a bull, the finest of at least three such figures from the site (the other two were excavated by Johann Georg Ramsauer).

Although archaeologists have sophisticated techniques for analyzing the technology of ancient artifacts and the physiological traits of ancient human remains, no tools exist that allow us to read ancient minds. There is abundant archaeological evidence that ritual and belief pervade all aspects of ancient life, yet the precise meaning of each symbol or image is difficult for us to discern.

Images of animals were especially plentiful during the Iron Age. They make up a broad spectrum of types—predatory or dangerous animals (birds of prey, snakes, lions, wild bulls, boar); domestic livestock (horses, cattle, sheep and rams, domestic fowl); and targets of the hunt (deer, waterfowl). They appear as jewelry or amulets, as images on weapons or armor, and as small figurines. It is clear that these animal images held great meaning in Iron Age culture, but whether they represented protective spirits, clan or family totems, shamans, ancestors, or all of the above is impossible for us to say. (T5131.2. Hillel S. Burger, photographer. Below: Drawing from Wells 1981, *The Emergence of an Iron Age Economy*, fig. 13b.)

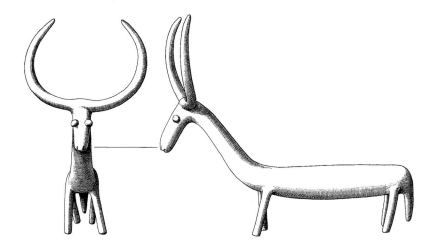

PLATE 13
Roman fluted glass bowl
40-77-40/12521
Vinica, Grave 314
Blown glass
Diameter 15.6 cm, height 4.2 cm

THESE ELEGANT GLASS BOWLS are of Roman rather than local manufacture. They were interred in a grave at Vinica that contained other Roman goods, further evidence of the changes in settlement and culture that followed the Roman conquest of the Adriatic (see also pl. 10).

These bowls are nearly as bright as they were on the day they were made. Glass is a chemically stable material and alters little, even after nearly two thousand years underground. In fact—as both the pattern of breakage and the field notes testify—the only significant damage to befall these bowls occurred at the hands of a careless fieldworker as they were being excavated. (Opposite and below: T3717. Hillel S. Burger, photographer.)

Roman fluted glass bowl
40-77-40/12522
Vinica, Grave 314
Blown glass
Diameter 10.2 cm, height 6.1 cm

PLATE 14
Bronze belt plate with repoussé
ornament
34-25-40/8516
Magdalenska gora, Tumulus V,
Grave 29
Sheet and cast bronze, iron rivets
Length 17.2 cm, width 7.7 cm

THIS BRONZE BELT PLATE is decorated with a frieze of running deer, similar in execution and style to the deer that decorate the situlae shown in the frontispiece and on page 9, and the scabbard plate reproduced on page 66. Depicted on a belt plate, which functioned as a piece of armor and protected the midriff, the deer presumably was significant to the wearer as a mark of identity or protection.

The belt plate is remarkable in that it had been repaired no fewer than five times (twice along the right edge, twice in the center, and once along the left edge) and had lost a considerable portion of its original length, yet remained in use. This repeated repair might be interpreted as a sign that the belt plate was the sole item of value in the wearer's possession—had it not come from the richest burial in all of the duchess's collections. Grave 29 in Tumulus V at Magdalenska gora contained a pair of male burials, nicknamed the "Hero Twins" because many of their accompanying objects were buried as matched pairs. The two men were accompanied by at least two pairs of horses, a pair of bronze cauldrons, another pair of bronze vessels, two pairs of iron spears, and a pair of bronze helmets (see pl. 20), along with several other spectacular items such as a fragmentary situla, a long iron sword, and at least two more belt plates (in good condition). It is clear that the value of this belt plate had little to do with the material value of the bronze and everything to do with the significance the owner placed on the object itself. (T5120.2. Hillel S. Burger, photographer. Below: Drawing from Hencken 1978, *The Iron Age Cemetery of Magdalenska gora in Slovenia*, fig. 140m.)

85

PLATE 15
Bronze situla with repoussé
ornament
34-25-40/8418
Magdalenska gora, Tumulus V,
Grave 6-7-7a
Sheet and cast bronze
Diameter 26 cm, height 28 cm

A SITULA IS A BUCKET-SHAPED VESSEL for mixing and serving wine. The social rituals and practices associated with wine drinking in Greece accompanied its introduction into central Europe, so in Iron Age Europe, as in the Greek world, wine was always diluted with water before being drunk. Because wine was a great luxury, the vessels used in serving and drinking it were often of high quality and value (see also pl. 3). Important chiefs owned vessels imported directly from Greece or its colonies. Lesser chiefs used vessels of local manufacture, in forms that imitated the Greek ones.

Numerous situlae are known from Mediterranean Europe. Many bear elaborate depictions of figures in low relief, a style associated with the Greek peninsula and the lands along the Adriatic. The scenes depict parades of animals and groups of people engaged in rituals whose meaning is only partly understood. The Peabody's Mecklenburg Collection includes two situlae from Magdalenska gora—this one, which is decorated, and one that is plain. A third situla, excavated by the duchess at Vače, is now at Oxford University's Ashmolean Museum.

Buried with the situla shown here were a helmet, a horse, two large bronze vessels, a suite of iron weapons, and a number of decorative personal items—beads, fibulae, dress fasteners, and so forth. Also in this burial were two long bronze rods of uncertain use. If these were roasting spits, they and the situla would suggest that this wealthy man held a public role in which the demonstration of hospitality played a part.

This situla is decorated with two horizontal registers separated by thin bands bearing a geometric or leaf motif. The top register depicts alternating stags and does; the lower register, a row of grazing rams and ewes. Beneath each animal is the same bifurcated leaf seen in the Vače Situla (see frontispiece and p. 9). (Opposite: T5146.2. Hillel S. Burger, photographer. Drawing from Hencken 1978, *The Iron Age Cemetery of Magdalenska gora in Slovenia*, fig. 111.)

PLATE 16

Left to right:

Iron socketed ax with bronze
inlay decoration on haft
34-25-40/8206
Magdalenska gora, Tumulus IV,
Grave 21
Iron, bronze
Length 19 cm, width 6 cm

Iron knife
34-25-40/8471
Magdalenska gora, Tumulus V,
Grave 15
Iron
Length 21.2 cm

Iron short spear
34-25-40/8209
Magdalenska gora, Tumulus IV,
Grave 21
Iron
Length 31.8 cm, width 4 cm

Iron long spear with bronze inlay
decoration on haft
34-25-40/8210
Magdalenska gora, Tumulus IV,
Grave 21
Iron, bronze
Length 45.5 cm, width 4 cm

IDEALLY, A WELL-ARMED WARRIOR at Stična or Magdalenska gora
had a suite of weapons consisting of a knife, a pair of spears (one usually
longer than the other), an ax, and a belt. The knife was the most commonly
carried weapon and doubled as a general-purpose tool—although the
knife in this photograph, with its sharp bend in the middle, was probably
intended specifically for fighting. The spearheads were once attached to
long shafts of oak (now deteriorated), and the ax was attached to its haft by
an open socket at the butt end. The belt (see pl. 17) served as both armor
and tool belt.

The long spear and the ax in this photograph are especially nicely
made, inlaid with bronze strips for decoration. (T5126.2. Hillel S. Burger,
photographer.)

PLATE 17
Bronze belt plate and
hanging straps
Belt plate, 34-25-40/8422; straps,
34-25-40/8436
Magdalenska gora, Tumulus V,
Grave 6-7-7a
Sheet and cast bronze
Belt plate, length 32.4 cm,
width 9.2 cm; straps,
length about 12 cm

A WARRIOR'S BELT had at its center a broad metal plate that not only held it closed but also protected the wearer's midriff. Plate armor was rare in the Iron Age, and most men made do with a belt plate and, probably, a leather tunic. Along the belt were riveted several rows of bronze straps ending in rings, from which hung the other tools and weapons—the knife, a whetstone, and on rare occasions a sword. (T5143.1. Hillel S. Burger, photographer.)

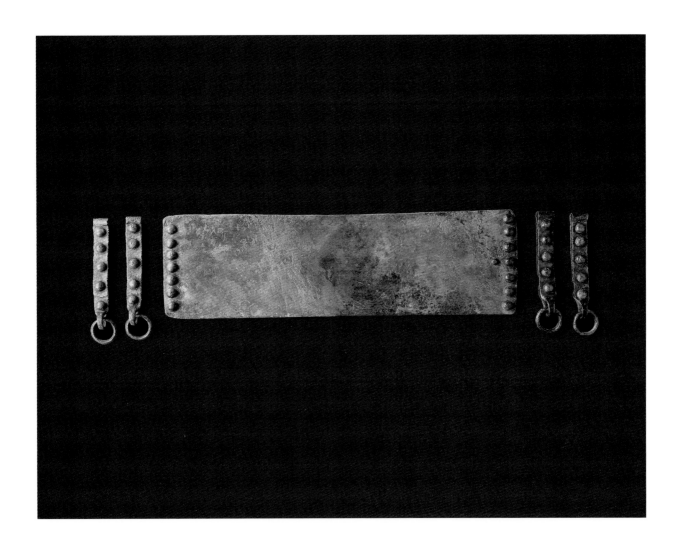

PLATE 18
Necklace of gold-plated bronze,
glass, and amber beads (modern
reconstruction)
40-77-40/13210
Stična, Tumulus II, isolated finds
Gold, bronze, glass, amber
Length (reconstruction) 22.0 cm

Necklace of colored glass beads
(modern reconstruction)
40-77-40/14602
Stična, Tumulus V, Grave 2
Glass, faience
Length (reconstruction) 13.0 cm

Necklace of clear, urn-shaped glass
beads (modern reconstruction)
40-77-40/13628
Stična, Tumulus V, Grave 11
Glass
Length (reconstruction) 14.5 cm

BEADS OF GOLD, AMBER, AND GLASS are not only decorative but also bear witness to the far-flung trade people engaged in at Stična. Gold is not native to the Stična region; the closest sources were probably in Austria to the north or around the Black Sea to the east. Gold is scarce in the Mecklenburg Collection, and these beads are made mostly of bronze, covered with a layer of gold foil to give them the appearance of gold.

Amber was traded to Stična from around the Baltic Sea, the main source of amber throughout central Europe. The "amber route" that led from the Baltic coast to the Adriatic had been established in early prehistory, and Stična and Magdalenska gora were fortunate to lie alongside this trade route. Iron Age people considered amber a powerful charm and especially associated it with women and girls. They greatly prized large chunks of amber and reworked or perforated them for reuse rather than discarding them.

Glass beads were made locally. A glass industry thrived all along the northern Adriatic coast, and artisans made beads in a variety of shapes, styles, and colors. Many of the pigments, such as copper (green), were available locally, but cobalt (blue) was not. This prized blue pigment is of uncertain origin, but it might have been imported from Asia Minor to the east.

The legacy of Iron Age glass production and trade continues today in the region around Venice, still famous for the artistry of its glassmakers. The continuity is so strong that some Venetian beads made for the colonial trade in the last two centuries, as well as modern African trade beads based on Venetian models, are almost indistinguishable from beads made along the Adriatic nearly two thousand years ago.

The strings of beads shown here are not authentic reconstructions. The strands that held the beads together disintegrated long ago, and the beads were found scattered loose in the burials at Stična. They were later strung together in patterns pleasing to modern eyes. (Opposite: T5129.2. Hillel S. Burger, photographer.)

EVEN THOUGH she had the modern advantage of photography, the duchess apparently had watercolor renderings made of some of her finds, imitating the style used by Ramsauer to portray his Hallstatt artifacts. Archaeologist Oscar Montelius mentions in a letter that she hired an artist, and there is even a photograph of the man at his easel, recording the excavations at Stična. Unfortunately, we do not know his name.

These watercolors show three strings of beads. The two strands on this page are of glass, and are similar in style to the colored glass beads shown in plate 18. The third string, opposite, features large pendants of amber, several of them perforated multiple times. These are three of only a handful of watercolor renderings that survived to attest to the artist's skill. If grave or site plans were made, they must have been lost sometime during the complex post-excavation history of the collection. (Opposite: T3703.1; below: T3704.1. Hillel S. Burger, photographer.)

95

PLATE 20
Bronze helmet, intact
34-25-40/8521
Magdalenska gora, Tumulus V,
Grave 29
Cast bronze
Length 27 cm, width 25.2 cm,
height 19.5 cm

Bronze helmet, crushed
34-25-40/8520
Magdalenska gora, Tumulus V,
Grave 29
Cast bronze
Length 31.5 cm, width 23.3 cm,
height 23.5 cm

THESE HELMETS, a matched pair, were found in the grave of the so-called Hero Twins (see pl. 14). One has survived intact, and the other has not. They date to about the fourth century B.C.

Although they are bare metal now, the helmets were once much more elaborate. The rims are decorated with the ubiquitous "eye" motif. The helmets are quite heavy, and a continuous row of small holes around the inner rim suggests that they were once lined with cloth or leather to ease the pressure on the wearer's head. Two pairs of loops on the underside of the brim were used to attach chinstraps. On the exterior, a small button in the front(?) and a loop in the back were used to attach a plume, probably of horsehair, in the Greek style. A similar helmet, with its long plume, is depicted in the middle register of the Vače Situla (see frontispiece and p. 9). (T5054.2. Hillel S. Burger, photographer.)

PLATE 21

Ceramic Este-style urn with
graphite band decoration
34-25-40/14039
Magdalenska gora, Tumulus VII,
Grave 34
Clay, graphite
Maximum diameter 27 cm,
height 28.4 cm

Ceramic footed bowl with lid
34-25-40/14309 and 14309.1 (lid)
Magdalenska gora, Tumulus X,
Grave 38
Clay
Maximum diameter 24 cm,
height (excluding lid) 29.2 cm

THESE LARGE CERAMIC VESSELS are known as urns more because of their shape than because of their function. The knobbed gray vessel (right) is characteristic of local pottery styles in the Carniola region. The red urn (left) is made in imitation of the style of the contemporary Este culture from across the Adriatic, on the Italian coast near Venice and the Po Valley. Nearly identical Este-style urns were also excavated at Vinica, even though Vinica was not inhabited until several centuries later. One characteristic of the Vinica "Tardy Hallstatt" style was the retention of anachronistic cultural traits many centuries after they had passed out of use in their place of origin.

On the Italian side of the Adriatic, vessels such as these were intended to hold cremated ashes, but at Stična and Magdalenska gora, the burial rite was inconsistent. Some burials in each tumulus were cremations; others were inhumations. Some of the cremations were placed in urns; others were not. This knobbed and lidded vessel accompanied an inhumation. (T3718.1. Hillel S. Burger, photographer.)

PLATE 22
Segmented bronze bracelets
34-25-40/14386A and 14386B
Magdalenska gora, Tumulus VII,
Grave 40
Bronze
14386A: Length 8.4 cm, width 8.2
cm, diameter 2.3 cm
14386B: Length 8.2 cm, width 8.2
cm, diameter 2.5 cm

THESE ORNAMENTS, along with those shown on pages 10 and 16, came from the grave of a woman of extraordinary wealth. She was buried wearing a total of four bronze bracelets, twenty-eight bronze ankle rings, six bronze neck rings (see p. 10), ten glass, amber, and bronze fibulae (including the four leech-shaped glass and bronze examples on this page), numerous glass and amber beads, and several bronze earrings, pendants, and hair ornaments. In addition to jewelry, her grave contained an iron awl, a bronze needle, and five clay spindle whorls. The woman would not have worn such a quantity of jewelry in daily life, but its inclusion en masse in her burial was a tangible manifestation of her status in her community.

Discovered at dusk, the grave was therefore excavated in some haste. Gustav Goldberg mentions in his notes, with some annoyance, that the duchess removed the objects faster than he was able to record them. The gathering darkness also prevented the two from photographing the excavated grave, but a visitor, a Professor Torres, made a partial sketch of the artifacts in situ (see p. 16). (Opposite: T5128.1; inset: T5144.2; below: T5142.1. Hillel S. Burger, photographer.)

Bronze fibulae with glass bows
34-25-40/14053.1 and 14053.2
Magdalenska gora, Tumulus VII, Grave 40
Glass, bronze
14053.1: Length 4.9 cm, width 2.8 cm, diameter 2.2 cm
14053.2: Length 6.8 cm, width 3.3 cm, diameter 2.6 cm

Opposite, inset:
Bronze fibulae with glass bows
34-25-40/14053.3 and 14053.4
Magdalenska gora, Tumulus VII, Grave 40
Glass, bronze
14053.3: Length 7.3 cm, width 2.5 cm, diameter 2.2 cm
14053.4: Length 7.1 cm, width 2.8 cm, diameter 2 cm

PLATE 23
Iron sword
34-25-40/8524
Magdalenska gora, Tumulus V,
Grave 42
Iron
Length 53.5 cm, width 3.6 cm

Folded iron sword with fragments
of iron scabbard
34-25-40/8596
Magdalenska gora, Tumulus V,
Grave 42
Iron
Estimated length when unfolded,
120 cm, width 8.0 cm

IRON SWORDS are rare in the Mecklenburg Collection and in Early Iron Age sites in general, the more common weapons being spears and axes. They became more common in the later part of the Iron Age as improvements in iron technology made possible the production of blades that were both sharp and durable.

These swords and fragments date to the latest part of the Magdalenska gora sequence. The incised bronze band–shaped mount and decorated iron chape (below) were part of the scabbard of a long sword that measured 88.5 cm when excavated (see drawing, opposite). The short sword in the photograph was part of the rich "Hero Twins" burial (pls. 14, 20). The burial containing the longer, folded sword is very late in date, nearly two centuries later than the main Magdalenska gora occupation, and was probably an intrusion into an old tumulus. Folded along the blade are the clearly preserved fragments of an iron scabbard.

The folded sword was deliberately destroyed, or "ritually killed," prior to burial. Destruction of the weapon for burial served several purposes. It removed the sword both symbolically and in fact from its role in the living world. Whereas an intact sword was valuable, a ruined sword was useless and would not tempt a looter to disturb the grave. Moreover, a sword (unlike other weapons) was believed to have an intrinsic power that was held in check by its owner while he lived (think Excalibur); folding and burying the sword with its owner negated its power, preventing its uncontrolled force from endangering the living. (Opposite: T5151.1; drawing from Hencken 1978, *The Iron Age Cemetery of Magdalenska gora in Slovenia*, fig. 125a; below: T5065.1. Hillel S. Burger, photographer.)

Bronze scabbard mount and decorated iron chape
34-25-40/8477
Magdalenska gora, Tumulus V, Grave 19-20
Iron, bronze, gold
Mount: Length 6.5 cm, width 6.0 cm
Chape: Length 6.0 cm, width 5.0 cm

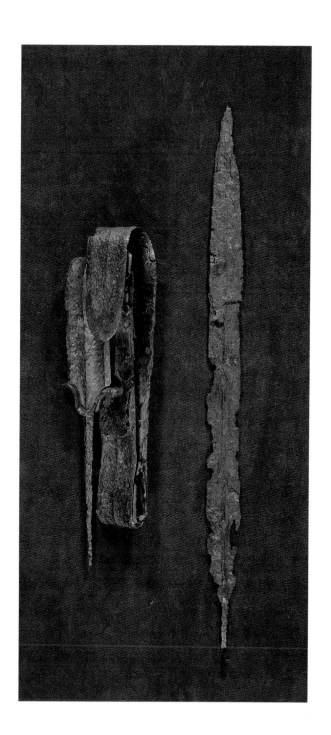

Bronze neck ring with fragments
of textile adhering
34-25-40/8619
Magdalenska gora, Tumulus V,
isolated finds
Bronze
Diameter 17.5 cm

FRAGMENTS OF TEXTILES and other organic materials are extremely rare in European archaeological sites. As a rule, the soils are too damp to allow for good preservation of such materials, and they deteriorate quickly. Still, it is likely that the bulk of the everyday objects used in prehistoric villages were made from organic materials—vessels and baskets of wood, reeds, and grasses; garments of cloth and leather; houses of timber and thatch. These materials were abundant, easy to obtain, and easy to fashion.

Perishable materials survive in only a handful of the Mecklenburg artifacts. For the most part, the use of organic materials can be inferred from the preserved inorganic components of the objects—spears that no longer have shafts, axes without hafts, belt plates without belts. The abundance of clothing pins and fasteners implies that the deceased were fully dressed for burial, but the garments have long since disintegrated.

Evidence for cloth in the collection is limited to five samples, including the two pictured here. In all cases the fragments were preserved only by contact with iron or bronze: as the metals oxidized, traces of their minerals infiltrated the fibers. In time, the minerals fully replaced the organic components but preserved the minute structures of the weaves and threads. (Opposite: T5148.1; right: T5057.2) Hillel S. Burger, photographer.

Bronze fibula with fragments
of textile adhering
40-77-40/13607
Stična, Tumulus V, Grave 7
Bronze
Length 10 cm, width 5.5 cm

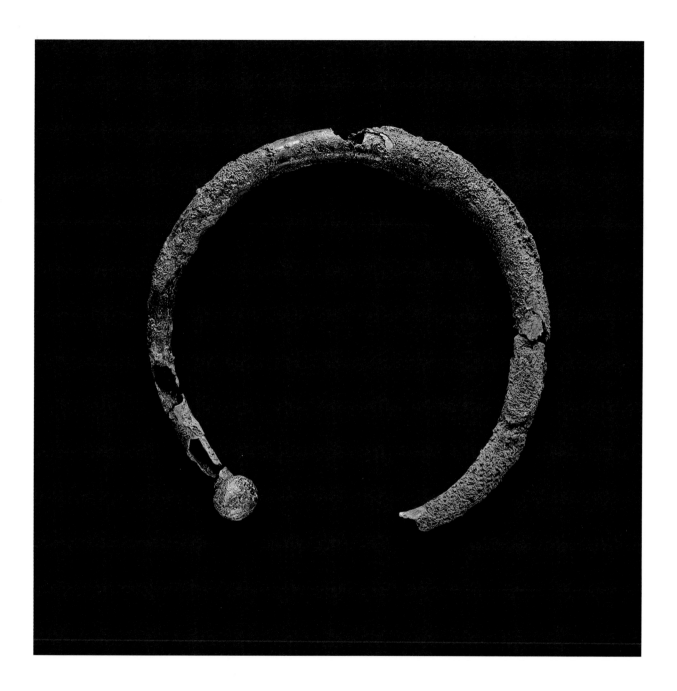

PLATE 25
Serpentine ("dragon") fibula
40-77-40/13447
Stična, Tumulus IV, Grave 32
Cast bronze and bronze wire
Length 9 cm

Serpentine fibula
40-77-40/9866
Hallstatt, Grave 5
Cast bronze and bronze wire
Length 8 cm

THE SERPENTINE FIBULA, one of the earliest forms of fibulae, was a simple wire bent into a loop, with one end broadened into a catch-plate. The form was short-lived and not particularly successful—it was fragile, its tension was weak in comparison with the coiled-spring fibula, and cloth would slide up around the bend to cover the bow. As in the smaller fibula pictured here, a small disc or knob at the bend was often added to keep the cloth in place.

Although serpentine fibulae were generally simple in form, occasionally they sported elaborate decorations. These decorated serpents are referred to as "dragons." The dragon fibula illustrated here bears an elaborate structure of knobs and cups that was affixed to the bow. An exquisite little bird keeps watch over the whole—as it presumably did over the person wearing the pin. (T5137.1. Hillel S. Burger, photographer.)

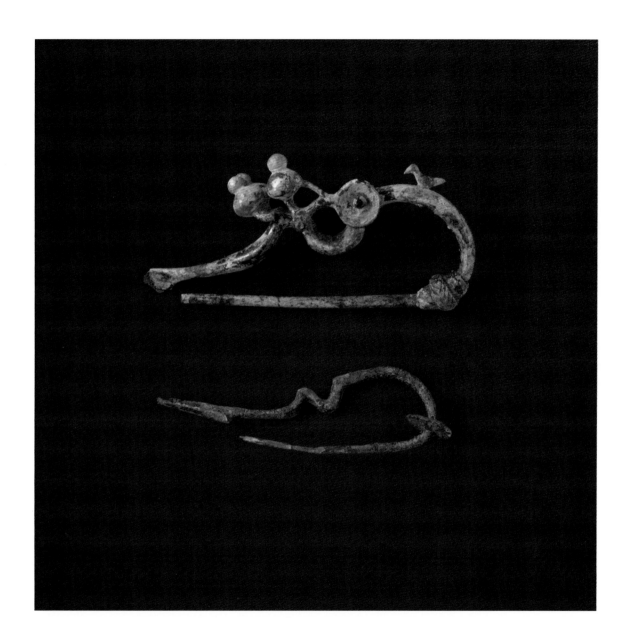

NOTES

1. Although the Peabody Museum owns the great majority of the Mecklenburg Collection, smaller parts of it reside in several European museums. The Narodni muzej Slovenije (National Museum of Slovenia) in Ljubljana, was given a part of the collection to retain as national patrimony when the remainder of the collection was approved for sale in 1930. The Ashmolean Museum at Oxford University purchased an auction lot (containing a situla excavated by the duchess at Vače) when the collection was offered for sale by Anderson Galleries (for details of both transactions, see the chapter "The Great War and Its Aftermath"). The Museum für Vor- und Frühgeschichte (Museum of Pre- and Early History) in Berlin owns the artifacts that the duchess gave to Kaiser Wilhelm II prior to World War I (see "A New Patron").

2. Information provided to the Peabody Museum from the records of the Staatsarchiv Schwerin, memo dated 27 June 1985 (Peabody Museum of Archaeology and Ethnology, Hugh Hencken Papers, Accession 995-18, Box 4, Folder 4.3). The memo names a succession of legal guardians; the order was annulled in May 1920.

3. Count Axel von Schwering (pseudonym), *The Berlin Court under William II* (London: Cassell, 1915). A publisher's note reads: "The work here presented is issued under an assumed name, in accordance with the expressed wish of the distinguished author." The memoir, which

chronicles life at the court of Kaiser Wilhelm II, takes a darker turn as the prospect of European war becomes imminent. "Count Axel" is presented as a close personal friend and confidant of the kaiser's; he nevertheless believes that the kaiser's ambitions have overtaken his judgment and that the war will end disastrously for Germany. By the end, it becomes clear that the book is addressed personally to Wilhelm, an extended suicide note as Axel takes his own life in protest of Germany's role in precipitating the war.

4. Schloss Wagensberg (modern Bogenšperk) is about thirty miles southeast of Ljubljana. The castle was built in 1511 for the Wagen family. Its primary significance in Slovene history is its association with the seventeenth-century historian and natural scientist Janez Vajkard Valvasour. Valvasour lived at Schloss Wagensberg during the time he wrote and illustrated his monumental work *The Glory of the Duchy of Carniola* (1689). The Windischgrätz family purchased Wagensberg in the mid-nineteenth century and remained there until the Italian occupation in 1943. The castle was turned into a museum in the 1970s, featuring displays on Valvasour and his work and on the natural and cultural history of Slovenia.

5. Rainer-Maria Weiss, "Des Kaisers Alte Funde," in Ingrid Griesa and Rainer-Maria Weiss, *Hallstattzeit* (Berlin: Staatlichen Museen zu Berlin, 1999), 49. Original in German; translated by the author.

6. *Chiefdom* is an imprecise word whose meaning occasions much debate among anthropologists. As a general rule, a chiefdom is a form of centralized political and social control. It is a political entity whose members do not necessarily share bonds of kinship. Social standing is hierarchical and hereditary, with chiefs at the top, an intermediate class of elites and warriors, and the laborers and craftsmen at the bottom. The chiefs profit from the labor of the farmers, craftsmen, and traders but are expected to provide defense and ritual intervention and to share (redistribute) the goods they acquire through gifts and feasts. In this way, chiefdoms are distinct from *tribes,* in which members are part of an extended family (clan) and share their goods with respect to age, lineage, and reciprocal benefit; and from *kingdoms,* which are highly stratified tribute systems in which redistribution of goods plays little part.

7. Weiss, "Des Kaisers Alte Funde," 51.

8. Ibid.

9. Ibid., 52.

10. Ibid.

11. Ibid., 50.

12. The duchess's improvements in the stratigraphic recording of her excavations took place within a context of rapid progress in scientific excavation techniques in both Europe and North America at this time. It is impossible to know whether or not stepping back the trenches

to expose the grave in plan was a solution that the duchess and Goldberg figured out for themselves, but at the very least it attests to the level of support and assistance she had from colleagues such as Montelius, who was himself in the forefront of the methodological developments in Europe.

13. Emil Vogt, "The Cemetery of Vinica (Weinitz) in Carniola," in Adolf Mahr, ed., *Prehistoric Grave Material from Carniola* (New York: American Art Association/Anderson Galleries, 1934), 47–56.

14. Johann Georg Ramsauer, "Die Altertums-Gräber vom Salzburg zu Hallstatt in Oberösterreich" (unpublished manuscript, circa 1863, Oxford University). Also, there is a facsimile edited by Karl Kromer, *Das Gräberfeld von Hallstatt,* Association Internationale d'Archéologie Classique, Monograph 1 (Florence: Sansoni, 1959).

15. This discussion is based in part on the evidence from Hallstatt itself and in part on information gained from other, more recent excavations of salt-mining sites in this area. Information about the skeletal changes comes from excavations at the Dürrnberg. Ernst Penninger, *Der Dürrnberg bei Hallein* (Munich: C. H. Beck, 1972).

16. Emperor Franz Josef to the Duchess of Mecklenburg, 16 September 1907, Peabody Museum of Archaeology and Ethnology, Mecklenburg Collection Archives (Accessions 34-25 and 40-77), Folder 1, no. 5. Original in German; translated by the author.

17. Diary of Josef Szombathy, 20 October 1907, in the collection of the Naturhistorisches Museum, Vienna, transcribed in Peter Wells, *The Emergence of an Iron Age Economy* (Cambridge, Mass.: American School of Prehistoric Research Bulletin 33, 1981), 17. The transcription is in German, from the original German and shorthand; translated by the author.

18. Ferdinand von Hochstetter, "Die neuesten Gräberfunde von Watsch und St. Margarethen in Krain und der Culturkreis der Halstätter Periode." *Denkschriften der Mathematisch-Naturwissenschaftliche Klasse, der Kaiserlichen Academie der Wissenschaften,* Vienna, Volume 47, 1883.

19. For the most recent information about this cuirass, see Rainer-Maria Weiss, "Der Brustpanzer von Stična–St. Veit," *Acta Praehistorica et Archaeologica* 25 (1993): 168–185. As Weiss points out, the cuirass was an incredibly rare find—only seven such breastplates are known (five of which are complete). Whether it was made in Greece itself, in a Greek provincial workshop, or in central Europe in imitation of a Greek form is not yet possible to say.

20. Goldberg arrived in Hamburg on 22 June 1913 and remained there for about a week. He was invited aboard the royal yacht, the *Hohenzollern,* to help the kaiser unpack the crates and to recount the excavation of their contents. He wrote in his memoirs: "I attended dinner on the ship. The major-domo, Count Platen, told me that my dining partner would be the Countess

Bassewitz, a lady-in-waiting of the empress. As soon as I had sat at her side, she began to speak eagerly about the Eberswald gold hoard and with the greatest expertise about the Lausitz culture, so that I asked her with astonishment how she had come by all this knowledge. 'My God!' she said, 'The kaiser force-feeds it to us every day!'" Goldberg's memoirs, cited in Weiss, "Des Kaisers Alte Funde," 60.

21. Kaiser Wilhelm II to the Duchess of Mecklenburg, 28 June 1913. Written aboard the imperial yacht *Hohenzollern* and delivered to the duchess at Wagensberg by Gustav Goldberg. Peabody Museum of Archaeology and Ethnology, Mecklenburg Collection Archives (Accessions 34-25 and 40-77), Folder 2, no. 1. Original in English.

22. The photographs, as well as the extant field documents and correspondence, are included in the Mecklenburg Collection Archives in the Peabody Museum (Accessions 34-25 and 40-77).

23. Letter cited in Weiss, "Des Kaisers Alte Funde," 61–62.

24. Déchelette's paper was later published as "Fouilles de Carniole," *Revue Archaeologique* 22 (1913).

25. Joseph Déchelette to the Duchess of Mecklenburg, 15 October 1913, Peabody Museum of Archaeology and Ethnology, Mecklenburg Collection Archives (Accessions 34-25 and 40-77), Folder 4, no. 2. Original in French; translated by the author.

26. Telegrams, Duchess of Mecklenburg to Oscar Montelius, 13–16 October 1913, Archives of the Swedish National Heritage Board. Originals in English.

27. Oscar Montelius to the Duchess of Mecklenburg, 16 October 1913, Peabody Museum of Archaeology and Ethnology, Mecklenburg Collection Archives (Accessions 34-25 and 40-77), Folder 3, no. 1. Original in German; translated by the author.

28. Telegram, Duchess of Mecklenburg to Oscar Montelius, 18 October 1913, Archives of the Swedish National Heritage Board. Original in English.

29. Kaiser Wilhelm II to the Duchess of Mecklenburg, 8 February 1914, Peabody Museum of Archaeology and Ethnology, Mecklenburg Collection Archives (Accessions 34-25 and 40-77), Folder 2, no. 3. Original in English.

30. Sandor Bökönyi, *Data on Iron Age Horses of Central and Eastern Europe,* American School of Prehistoric Research Bulletin 25 (Cambridge, Mass.: Peabody Museum of Archaeology and Ethnology, 1968).

31. Mixing wine with water was considered a hallmark of civilized Greek behavior, in contrast to the barbarian practice of drinking undiluted wine. For example, in Herodotus, *Histories,* Book 6: "[Cleomenes'] own countrymen declare that his madness proceeded not from any supernatural cause whatever, but only from the habit of drinking wine unmixed with

water, which he learnt of the Scyths. When the Scyths came to Sparta on this errand Cleomenes was with them continually; and growing somewhat too familiar, learnt of them to drink his wine without water, a practice which is thought by the Spartans to have caused his madness. Still to this day the Spartans . . . have been accustomed, when they want to drink purer wine than common, to give the order to fill 'Scythian fashion.'"

32. Curators at the Narodni muzej Slovenije also had some opportunity to study and document the artifacts prior to the sale. Rajko Ložar, "Predzgodovina Slovenije, posebej Kraniske, v luci zbirke Mecklenburg" [Prehistory of Slovenia, particularly the Kraijna, as seen by the Mecklenburg Collection], *Glasnik, muzejskega drustava Slovenio* 15 (1934): 5–91.

33. Advising Mahr on the contents of the collection and contributing to the catalogue were J. M. de Navarro (University of Cambridge), Balduin Saria (University of Laibach [Ljubljana]), Ferenc de Tompa (National Museum of Hungary, Budapest), Emil Vogt (Swiss Federal Museum, Zurich), Raymond Lantier (Musée des Antiquités, St. Germaine-en-Laye), and Gero von Merhart (University of Marburg).

34. Hugh Hencken to Donald Scott, 28 May 1933, Peabody Museum of Archaeology and Ethnology, Mecklenburg Collection Archives, Accession File 34–25.

35. Notes and Comments: "The Carniola Treasure." *Art and Archaeology* 34, no. 4 (Nov.–Dec. 1933): 319–320.

36. The present author is in the process of organizing the catalogue of the Vinica artifacts as a companion to the previously published volumes on Magdalenska gora (Hencken 1978) and Stična (Wells 1981), to be published by the Peabody Museum Press. The volume is also intended to include the artifacts from the numerous small sites excavated by the duchess and articles about recent research on the Mecklenburg Collection.

37. Weiss, "Der Brustpanzer," 168–185; and Rainer-Maria Weiss, "Ein reiches Kriegergrab aus Magdalenska gora: Neue Erkenntnisse zu einem alten Fund," *Acta Praehistorica et Archaeologica* 28 (1996): 40–58.

Suggested Reading

For information in this book, I am indebted to several earlier publications about the Mecklenburg Collection and the Duchess of Mecklenburg. I encourage readers to seek these out for a treatment of the subject in greater depth.

There are five primary publications on the Mecklenburg Collection. The first is the auction catalogue, *Prehistoric Grave Material from Carniola Excavated in 1905–14 by H. H. the late Duchess Paul Friedrich of Mecklenburg,* edited by Adolf Mahr (New York: American Art Association/Anderson Galleries Inc., 1934). Although somewhat out of date now, it is a read-able overview of the collection as a whole, supplemented by in-depth scholarly assessments of the cultural significance of the artifacts in the context of central European archaeology. The scholars who contributed to the volume were among the most accomplished of their time.

There also exist four catalogues previously published by the Peabody Museum: Sandor Bökönyi's *Data on Iron Age Horses of Central and Eastern Europe* and Lawrence Angel's *Human Skeletal Material from Slovenia* (both published in American School of Prehistoric Research [ASPR] Bulletin 25, Peabody Museum of Archaeology and Ethnology, 1968); Hugh Hencken's *The Iron Age Cemetery of Magdalenska gora* (ASPR Bulletin 32, 1978); and Peter Wells's *The Emergence of an Iron Age Economy* (ASPR Bulletin 33, 1981). These works describe each find in detail, within the context of its tumulus and grave group. The catalogues are supplemented by syntheses of archaeological research in the region and discussions of the roles these sites played within their cultural context.

Hencken and Wells have also published articles on various aspects of the collections. Especially interesting are Wells's "The Excavations at Stična in Slovenia by the Duchess of Mecklenburg, 1905–1914" (*Journal of Field Archaeology*, vol. 5, 1978), and "How the Peabody Museum Acquired the Mecklenburg Collection," Hencken's personal account of his dealings with Anderson Galleries (*Symbols*, Peabody Museum, Fall 1981).

For those who read German, information about Kaiser Wilhelm II's archaeological collections and about the Königliche Museum für Völkerkunde in Berlin can be found in the catalogue *Hallstattzeit,* by Ingrid Griesa and Rainer-Maria Weiss (Museum für Vor- und Frühgeschichte–Staatlichen Museen zu Berlin, 1999). It offers an overview of the contents, history, and significance of the museum's Early Iron Age collections. I am greatly indebted to this work for the information about the duchess's early excavations and her involvement in the Secret Stična Project.

Finally, Philip Mason wrote a review of recent archaeology in Slovenia: *The Early Iron Age of Slovenia* (British Archaeological Reports, International Series 643, 1996). He synthesized many decades of research, much of it originally published in Slovene, making it available to readers in English.

Many of the sources I used for this book, especially much of the correspondence, have not been published. Letters from the staff of the Berlin Museum für Völkerkunde—Wilhelm von Bode, Friedrich Rathgen, and Alfred Götze—are held in the archives of that institution. The passages I quoted were published in Weiss's article "*Des Kaisers Alte Funde*" in the *Hallstattzeit* catalogue. Letters to the duchess from her colleagues and cousins—Montelius, Déchelette, Viollier, Emperor Franz Josef, and Kaiser Wilhelm II—as well as the letters of Hugh Hencken, are in the Archives of the Peabody Museum of Archaeology and Ethnology (Accessions 34–25 and 40–77). Telegrams and letters from the duchess to Montelius were provided by the Archives of the Swedish National Heritage Board.

Readable general summaries of European prehistory are surprisingly few. Most are burdened with an overabundance of Druids and bleeding sacrificial victims. For readers who would like a good general background on European cultures in the Iron Age, the following books might prove interesting:

Dale M. Brown, editor

1994   *The Celts: Europe's People of Iron.* New York: Time–Life Books, Lost Civilizations
series.
"Lost Civilizations" is one of the better archaeological series from Time–Life,
dwelling less on the mysteries and secrets and more on the archaeology, scientists,
and research. This book includes good summary essays on historical and literary
sources, daily and religious life, conflict with the Romans, and artwork. As in all
Time–Life books, the graphics are excellent. It also contains a short pictorial essay
on the Duchess of Mecklenburg and her excavations.

Champion, Timothy, Clive Gamble, Stephen Shennan, and Alasdair Whittle

1984   *Prehistoric Europe.* London: Academic Press.
Prehistoric Europe is a textbook intended for teaching European archaeology at the
college level. It provides a comprehensive chronological treatment for the whole of
temperate Europe, from the earliest hominid populations through the coming of the
Romans. The authors compare developments in different regions of Europe during
each cultural period. The focus is primarily on economic and social development
rather than on works of art.

Cunliffe, Barry

1986   *The Celtic World.* New York: Greenwich House.
Cunliffe's book is a densely illustrated tour through all aspects of Celtic culture.
Although his own expertise is in prehistory, his discussion continues beyond the
Roman conquest to the Celtic culture of medieval Ireland, to the literary renaissance
of the early twentieth century, and finally to nationalist movements and modern
Celtic revivals in the culture and politics of Ireland, Scotland, Wales, and Brittany.

Kruta, Venceslas, editor

1999   *The Celts.* New York: Rizzoli.
This is a massive volume, nearly eight hundred pages long, with more than a thousand fine photographs. It was produced as a catalogue to accompany a monumental
exhibit of archaeological treasures at the Palazzo Grassi in Venice in 1991. Its more
than sixty articles on all aspects of Celtic life, art, literature, settlement, and beliefs
were written by leading scholars in each field.

Wells, Peter S.

1984 *Farms, Villages, and Cities: Commerce and Urban Origins in Late Prehistoric Europe.*
Ithaca, N.Y.: Cornell University Press.

Wells looks at trade and commerce as a medium for understanding the development of towns and cities in pre-Roman Europe. The development of centralized "urban" sites as centers of trade and manufacturing paralleled the development of centralized polities, because control over trade routes and commodities was an important source of chiefly authority.

Wells, Peter S.

2001 *Beyond Celts, Germans, and Scythians: Archaeology and Identity in Iron Age Europe.*
London: Duckworth.

Prehistorians and historians have used labels such as "Celt" and "German" as convenient means of differentiating the various groups that inhabited Europe in the Iron Age. It is usually forgotten that these names came to us through Classical sources and likely were not ethnic distinctions that native peoples themselves recognized. Wells uses these names as a point of departure to discuss the construction of identity among ancient peoples and to investigate these distinctions through the medium of their material culture.